CULTURES OF THE WORLD
Cyprus

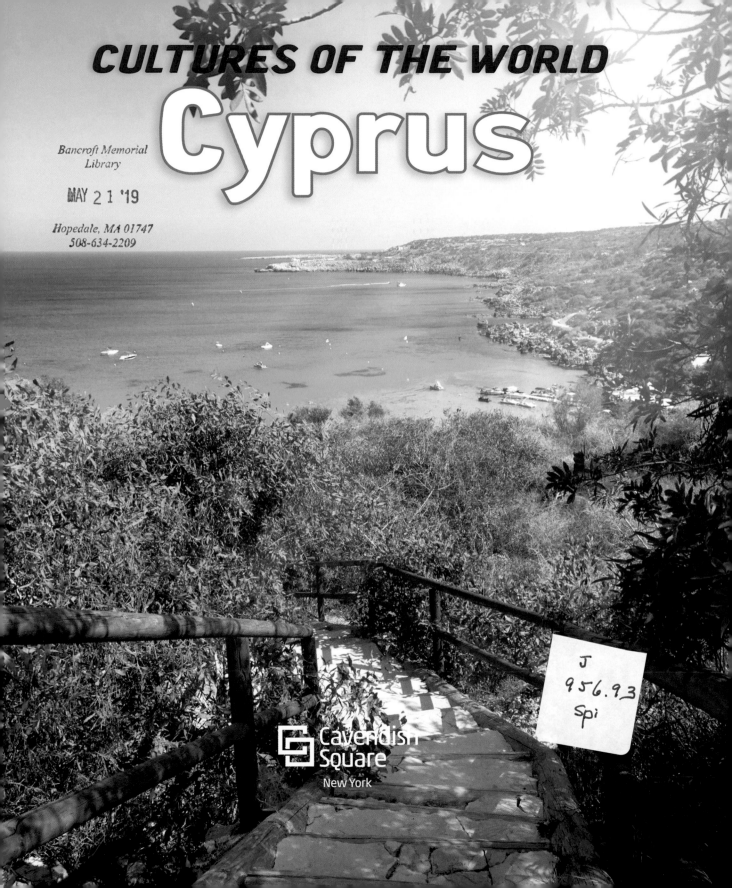

Cavendish
Square
New York

Published in 2019 by Cavendish Square Publishing, LLC
243 5th Avenue, Suite 136, New York, NY 10016

Third Edition

Website: cavendishsq.com

This publication represents the opinions and views of the author based on his or her personal experience, knowledge, and research. The information in this book serves as a general guide only. The author and publisher have used their best efforts in preparing this book and disclaim liability rising directly or indirectly from the use and application of this book.

All websites were available and accurate when this book was sent to press.

Library of Congress Cataloging-in-Publication Data

Names: Spilling, Michael, author. | Spilling, Jo-Ann, author. | Young-Brown, Fiona, author.
Title: Cyprus / Michael and Jo-Ann Spilling, and Fiona Young-Brown.
Description: First edition. | New York : Cavendish Square, [2020] |
Series: Cultures of the world | Includes bibliographical references and index. |
Audience: Grades 6 and up.
Identifiers: LCCN 2018044267 (print) | LCCN 2018045068 (ebook) |
ISBN 9781502647337 (ebook) | ISBN 9781502647320 (library bound)
Subjects: LCSH: Cyprus--Juvenile literature.
Classification: LCC DS54.A3 (ebook) | LCC DS54.A3 S65 2018 (print) |
DDC 956.93--dc23
LC record available at https://lccn.loc.gov/2018044267

Editorial Director: David McNamara
Editor: Kristen Susienka
Copy Editor: Nathan Heidelberger
Associate Art Director: Alan Sliwinski
Designer: Jessica Nevins
Production Coordinator: Karol Szymczuk
Photo Research: J8 Media

Printed in the United States of America

$ 29.65

CONTENTS

CYPRUS TODAY

THE ISLAND OF CYPRUS IS THE THIRD-LARGEST ISLAND IN THE Mediterranean Sea (after Sicily and Sardinia). It is located in the far eastern part of the Mediterranean. Its proximity to Greece, Turkey, and Syria makes it of strategic importance. Culturally, historically, and politically, it has often served as a bridge between Europe and the Middle East. It continues to do so today, but it is also a popular tourist destination, attracting hundreds of thousands of visitors each year with its beaches and traditional village life.

A DIVERSE HISTORY

Because of its location, Cyprus has a rich and varied history, one of occupation by a variety of different peoples. Archaeological evidence suggests that the first settlers lived here during the Neolithic period, some eight thousand years ago. However, they died out, leaving the island uninhabited for two thousand years. It was eventually resettled, and thus began a centuries-long power struggle between Greece and Turkey that some might say continues to this day. The island was under various periods of

The history of Cyprus and Great Britain are intertwined.

rule—Greek, Assyrian, Egyptian, Roman, Arab, and Byzantine—all long before the Middle Ages. During the Crusades, ownership changed hands several times until it became part of the Lusignan kingdom, eventually ruled by Venice. Then, in 1571, it fell to the Turkish-ruled Ottoman Empire. Thousands of Turks settled on the island, and for the next three centuries, it was largely unnoticed by the outside world.

That changed in 1878, when the British took over. They went on to fully annex the island during World War I. Cyprus became an official British colony, and with that came closer ties to Western Europe. Cyprus entered an economic boom period.

Despite Cyprus's relative distance from Greece (compared to the much closer Turkey), it owes much of its history and culture to Greek influence. Cypriots of Greek origin have historically been the majority population group. However, a sizable Turkish population means that there has been some ethnic conflict. As the Greek nationalist movement rose after World War II, so tensions between the two groups rose, reaching a peak when civil war broke out in the late 1950s. In 1960, Britain granted Cyprus its independence, but the ethnic divisions between Greeks and Turks continued. For example, even today, government seats are divided along ethnic lines and only a Greek Cypriot can hold the office of president.

After a Greek coup d'etat and a Turkish invasion in 1974, the island of Cyprus became divided. In the south is the Republic of Cyprus. To the north is the Turkish Republic of Northern Cyprus (TRNC), only officially recognized by Turkey. For more than forty years, the two have existed side by side, divided by politics and ethnicity. Both sides have expressed a desire for a solution, but despite repeated talks, it seems neither can agree on what that solution should look like. Turkish Cypriots want better inclusion, while Greek Cypriots express a fear of ceding too much power to Turkey. A referendum held in 2004 failed to bring about an agreement. The current presidents of both north and south say they seek reunification, but whether they can achieve it remains unlikely in the minds of many.

A THRIVING NATION

Although the divisions remain, Cyprus is, in many ways, thriving. The island may lack many natural resources, but it has found ways to make up for that, establishing itself as an important regional center for shipping imports and exports, and for banking. The latter proved to be a weakness in the economic decline of 2009. The Greek banks collapsed, and with them went many of the investments that Cyprus held. But the island proved resilient, working through a bailout program. As of 2018, Cyprus seemed to be recovering well. Unemployment rates were dropping once again, and economic growth was rebounding.

One strong contribution to the economy in both the north and the south is tourism. Tourism now provides a large portion of the annual gross domestic product, or GDP. Cyprus has only a few large towns or cities, but their coastal locations have made them attractive. Large amounts of real estate investment have created hotels, resorts, and other amenities designed to attract the many who travel here each year, mainly from Europe and Turkey. Yet Cyprus has more to offer than beaches and nightclubs. The island is rich in flora and fauna, with many species that cannot be found anywhere else.

In spite of the country's turmoil, past and ongoing, it is the Cypriot people who are the strength of the nation. Fiercely proud of their identity and traditions, they are known for their welcoming, hospitable nature. Through dance, music, food, and festivals, the people of Cyprus endure and prosper.

The traditions of Cyprus remain a strong feature of modern life.

GEOGRAPHY

Mountains surround the edge of the city of Limassol.

1

N THE FAR EASTERN PART OF THE Mediterranean, just 40 miles (64 kilometers) from Turkey, lies the island of Cyprus. It has a total land area of 3,571 square miles (9,251 square kilometers). Sixty miles (97 km) to the east is Syria, while mainland Greece is 480 miles (772 km) to the northwest. From the easternmost tip of Cape Andreas to Cape Arnauti in the west is a distance of 140 miles (225 km). The island is only 60 miles (97 km) wide. One range of mountains, the Kyrenia, lies along the northern coast. The Troodos Mountains are near the center of the island. A large plain divides the two. Since 1974, the island has been divided politically between the Turkish north (about 36 percent of the land area) and the Greek south (the remaining 64 percent).

Cyprus has the third-largest population of any Mediterranean island, with about 1.2 million people living there.

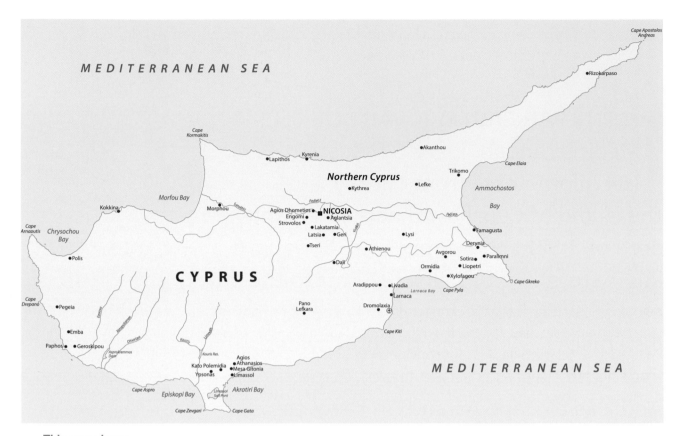

MEDITERRANEAN SEA

Cape Apostolos Andreas

•Rizokarpaso

Cape Kormakitis

•Akanthou

Kyrenia Trikomo•

•Lapithos *Cape Elaia*

Northern Cyprus •Lefke *Ammochostos*

•Kythrea *Bay*

Morfou Bay Agios Dhometios• ■NICOSIA

Morphou Engomi• •Aglantsia

Kokkina• Strovolos• •Famagusta

Cape Arnaoutis •Lakatamia Derynia•

Chrysochou Bay Latsia• •Geri •Lysi Avgorou

•Tseri •Athienou Sotira• •Paralimni

•Polis Ormidia •Liopetri

CYPRUS •Dali •Xylofagou

Cape Drepano Aradippou• •Livadia *Cape Gkreko*

•Pegeia •Larnaca *Larnaca Bay* *Cape Pyla*

Pano Dromolaxia•

•Emba Lefkara

Paphos• •Geroskipou *Cape Kiti*

Agios MEDITERRANEAN SEA

Athanasios•

Kato Polemidia• •Mesa-Gitonia

Ypsonas• •Limassol

Cape Aspro *Episkopi Bay* *Akrotiri Bay*

Cape Zevgari *Cape Gata*

This map shows some of the major features of Cyprus, including its main cities and towns, its rivers, and its bays.

PEAKS AND VALLEYS

Cyprus has two major mountain ranges—the Troodos, formed from molten rock beneath the ocean, and the Kyrenia, part of the Alpine-Himalayan chain that runs through the eastern Mediterranean.

The Troodos Mountains stretch from the northwest coast for about 50 miles (80 km) to Stavrovouni Peak (2,260 feet / 689 meters), which lies about 12 miles (19 km) from the southern coast. At 6,401 feet (1,951 m), Mount Olympus, sometimes known as Mount Troodos, is Cyprus's highest peak. On a clear winter day, there is a fantastic view from the northern slopes of Mount Olympus across Morphou Bay to the faraway Toros Mountains in Turkey. In contrast to the Kyrenia Mountains, the foothills and valleys of the Troodos Mountains are undulating and spacious. Two of the most beautiful valleys are the Marathasa and Solea, which cut into the northern slopes of the range. The valleys and folds of the hills conceal a huge number of villages, the highest of which is Prodromos, at 4,659 feet (1,420 m) above sea level.

Hugging the northern coast of Cyprus is the narrow, 100-mile-long (161 km) Kyrenia mountain range, which is also known as the Pentadaktylos ("five-fingered") range.

Lying between the two mountain ranges is the flat, low-lying Mesaoria Plain, which stretches from the city of Famagusta on the east coast to Morphou Bay in the west. In the center of the plain lies Nicosia, which is the capital of Cyprus. Dubbed the breadbasket of Cyprus, the Mesaoria Plain is the main cereal-growing area of the island, though only half of the land is irrigated.

The Kouris Dam is the largest in Cyprus and creates the scenic Kouris Reservoir.

The panhandle-shaped area of northeastern Cyprus is known as the Karpas Peninsula. The peninsula is remote and unspoiled, and it is an unpolluted, rich source of marine and bird life.

WATERWAYS

All of the island's major rivers originate in the Troodos Mountains. The largest, the Pedieos, flows east toward Famagusta Bay. Along with the Yialias, it irrigates much of the Mesaoria Plain. Other major rivers include the Karyotis, which flows north to Morphou Bay, and the Kouris, which flows south toward Episkopi Bay. Much of Cyprus's distinctive appearance comes from the valleys created by these rivers, with their deep, gravel beds. All the rivers, which are dry in the summer months, rely on winter rainfall. However, during sudden summer thunderstorms, some of the wadis (the Arabic term for valleys or streambeds that are dry for part of the year) can turn into raging torrents in under an hour.

On the south coast, two large saltwater lakes have formed near the towns of Limassol and Larnaca, from which the lakes take their names. These lagoons are a rich habitat for bird life, particularly in December and April, when birds migrate between Europe and the Nile Delta.

WEATHER PATTERNS

Cyprus has an intense Mediterranean climate marked by strong seasonal differences. Summer lasts from June to September, while winter lasts from November to March. Spring and autumn are short and are characterized by rapid changes in climate and an equally fast transformation of local plant life. Summers are hot and dry, but not humid. The central plain is usually the hottest, with temperatures averaging 100 degrees Fahrenheit (38 degrees Celsius) in Nicosia. Winters are mild, and the weather varies, with average temperatures a cool 40 to 59°F (4.4—15°C). The higher reaches of the Troodos Mountains experience several weeks of below-freezing nighttime temperatures in the winter. Rain generally occurs between October and March, with average annual rainfall of about 19 inches (48 centimeters). The island's agriculture is dependent on this rainfall, which is often unreliable. The mountain areas receive far more rain than the Mesaoria Plain. Average annual rainfall in Nicosia, for example, is only 13 inches (34 cm), while in the Troodos Mountains, it can be nearly 31 inches (79 cm). Over the past thirty years or so, rainfall levels have been decreasing in Cyprus. The annual rainfall in the Troodos Mountains used to be as high as 10 inches (25 cm) more than current estimates.

PLANT LIFE

As one of the island's major natural resources, the forests of Cyprus have been extensively exploited for many centuries. This has occurred for economic reasons, because the local people needed wood for export and land for farming. At one time, both the plains and mountains of Cyprus were forested. Today, roughly 18.8 percent of the island is still covered in forest. As early as 400 BCE, the island's rulers placed the local cedar forests under protection, but despite this, the island's forests have continued to be plundered by both conquerors and locals alike. Today the remaining forests are high in the Troodos and Kyrenia mountain ranges. In the 1990s and 2000s, the forestry department tried to stop the loss of forests with extensive replanting. Thanks to these reforestation efforts, forested land has been growing by roughly 2,965 acres (1,200 hectares) per year.

Cyprus is a flower-lover's dream. It is home to some 1,800 species, with more than 150 species of grass. During spring and summer, the countryside is alive with color. So far, 140 of the nation's plants have been identified as endemic, meaning that they are only found in Cyprus.

One of the most common native flowering plants on Cyprus is the orchid. Its popularity with gardeners around the world helps to make Cyprus a popular destination for tourists. Approximately fifty different species of orchid have been discovered here to date, and some are much more difficult to find than others.

The most likely place to find a variety of orchids is Akamas; at least half of the identified varieties grow there. The cape is where you might catch a glimpse of Cyprus's rare lax-flowered orchid, recognizable by its tiny purple blooms. Examples of other species growing here are the Argolian bee orchid (also known as the late spider orchid), the small dotted orchid, the Cyprus bee orchid, and the Orchis troodi. *While many are subspecies of other types of orchid, botanists believe they have now evolved into separate species in their own right because of Cyprus's isolated island location.*

The most common tree of the Troodos range is the Aleppo pine, which makes up the majority of all forests in Cyprus. In the upper reaches of the mountains, black pine can also be found. The pine forests are hardy and can resist the extremes of heat and cold. In the Troodos valleys, golden oak and willow can be found. As on many Mediterranean islands, cypress, eucalyptus, and juniper trees are common. The most famous tree in Cyprus is the cedar. However, today cedar trees only grow within the Paphos Forest on the slopes of Mount Tripylos, in the southwest area of the island.

Extensive scrub covers the foothills and low-lying areas that are not under cultivation. The scrub is made up of bulky, thorny bushes. The mastic shrub is very common, as are the turpentine tree and the strawberry tree. Rock rose bushes grow over the dry, sun-drenched hills, and can even be found on slopes

The Cyprus mouflon is recognizable by its large, curled horns.

high in the Kyrenia range. The southern and western slopes of the Troodos are extensively planted with grapevines, while orange groves dominate the area around Morphou Bay. Other cultivated trees include olive, carob, walnut, lemon, grapefruit, fig, date palm, and pomegranate. The Akamas Peninsula is home to hundreds of species of plants, including Aleppo pines, cypress, Phoenician junipers, and carob, oak, and caper trees.

WILDLIFE

Domestic animals, such as donkeys and oxen, are still a part of village life and are used for pulling carts and plows. Wild donkeys also roam the Karpas Peninsula. However, wild animals are now rare. The only large wild animal still living in Cyprus is the *agrino*, or mouflon, a kind of wild sheep. Recognizable by its large curly horns, and notable for the fact that it is only found on Cyprus, the mouflon is a symbol for the nation. It is under strict protection in restricted areas of the Paphos and Troodos regions. Once an endangered species, the mouflon is still rather rare. But it is a success story for Cypriot wildlife conservation. Recent estimates place the animal's numbers at about three thousand, compared with just three hundred some fifty years ago.

Small game is abundant but aggressively hunted, and foxes, hedgehogs, and shrews can be found all over the island. In contrast to much of the Mediterranean, sheep and goats are rare.

In classical times, snakes were so common that the island was named Orphiussa, which means "the abode of snakes." Now snakes are relatively rare. North of Paphos, the beaches of Cape Lara have become famous for nesting loggerhead and green sea turtles. These rare, protected species also nest on the beaches of the Karpas Peninsula. Cyprus is home to many lizards because its high temperatures and dry climate provide an ideal environment for them. The country's lizards include the impressive starred agama, which grows to a length of 12 inches (30 cm). It lives in rocky crevices and stone walls. The southern slopes of the Kyrenia Mountains are home to the

TURTLE CONSERVATION: A CYPRUS SUCCESS STORY

The western coast of the Paphos district is one of the last nesting grounds in the Mediterranean for green and loggerhead sea turtles. Both species require dry land to lay their eggs, so they choose deserted, sandy beaches for this purpose. In Cyprus, the turtles nest every two to three years from early June to mid-August. Each turtle lays about one hundred eggs every two weeks. The eggs are buried below the sand surface. The hatchlings emerge seven weeks later and instinctively dash for the sea, which they recognize from reflected moonlight or starlight. Sometimes artificial lights from taverns, hotels, and flashlights distract the newborn turtles,

causing them to move the wrong way and later die of dehydration. Tourist development has narrowed the choice of realistic breeding grounds for turtles, and popular nesting places can no longer be used. Once in the water, the hatchlings are easy prey for seals, sharks, and other large fish. On land, the eggs are sometimes dug up and eaten by foxes. As a result, it is estimated that only one in every one thousand eggs develops into an adult. Sea turtles only reach maturity fifteen to thirty years after hatching.

By the 1970s, surveys indicated an alarming drop in the turtle population. In fact, they had been hunted almost to extinction in the early part of the nineteenth century. In 1978, just three hundred turtle nests remained. The Cypriot government set up a project around Cape Lara to try to reverse the decline. The beaches around Cape Lara are off-limits to tourists every summer, when volunteers search the beaches for eggs. If a nest is judged to be poorly sited, the eggs are dug up and moved to a better location with anti-fox wire mesh. The Lara project has yielded good results.

In August 2018, the number of nests in Cyprus had increased to 1,100. Loggerhead turtles are currently vulnerable, or have a limited population, but green turtles are still listed as endangered. The news that the nest population is growing is encouraging to conservationists, who have worked hard to help the population grow in Cyprus and around the world. The most recent count of two hundred to three hundred female green turtles in Cyprus offers hope that the species may soon thrive there again.

blunt-nosed viper, and climbers occasionally have unwelcome encounters with these ledge-dwelling reptiles. Chameleons also live in Cyprus.

Bird life in Cyprus is varied and interesting. Nearly 400 different species of birds have been found on the island, most of which migrate. Every autumn, nearly 150 million birds pass through Cyprus to various migration destinations. One hundred million soar through Cyprus's skies during spring migration. The remote and undeveloped Karpas Peninsula is a natural, unpolluted habitat for most of the island's birds, and along with the Akamas Peninsula on the west coast, it is one of the few wild places left in Cyprus. More than 160 bird species, 12 mammals, 20 reptiles, and 16 butterfly species have been identified in the Akamas area, including falcons, turtledoves, crested larks, Cyprus warblers, and scops owls. Around the salt lakes of southern Cyprus, flamingos, herons, spoonbills, geese, and ducks can be seen. The salt lakes are an ideal habitat for brine shrimp, which make perfect food for flamingos. The Gönyeli Reservoir, on the northern edge of Nicosia, is a good place to see migrating birds.

More northern species, such as pigeons, wagtails, blackbirds, finches, and larks, visit the island in winter. Rock rose warblers, whitethroats, blue rock thrushes, coal tits, wrens, corn buntings, and sparrows are among the birds that nest in Cyprus. The rocky coastal crags of the Kyrenia Mountains are home to griffon vultures, hawks, peregrine falcons, and kestrels. The magnificent griffon vulture has a wingspan of 8 feet (2.5 m).

POPULATION CENTERS

Cypriots are traditionally rural people, and the village is the center of their lives. A steady drift of population to the towns began early in the twentieth century. This accelerated after the Turkish invasion of the island in 1974 and the consequent need to resettle many refugees in the southern part of the island. Before 1974, only six places were listed as towns—settlements of more than five thousand people—and six hundred villages were recorded. These six towns—Nicosia, Limassol, Larnaca, Paphos, Famagusta, and Kyrenia—are still the main urban settlements in Cyprus today. They are also the administrative centers for the island's six districts. One result of the Turkish invasion is that the southern, Greek portion of Cyprus is far more populated than the northern,

Turkish area. Many of the Cypriots who fled to the south settled around the towns of Limassol, Larnaca, and Paphos, which have grown rapidly since then. Nicosia, the capital, remains the only large inland settlement. It is rare for an island capital not to lie on the coast.

NICOSIA, the capital of Cyprus, is a divided city, with the northern portion occupied by Turks and the larger, southern section occupied by Greeks. The capital of Cyprus does not even have a common name—the Turks call it Lefkoşa, while the Greeks call it Lefkosia. Nicosia is an old name that was given to the city by European conquerors. The city has been divided since 1964, when communal violence between Turks and Greeks caused the British to divide the city. Around 269,000 people live in the Greek portion of the city, while an estimated 97,000 live in the Turkish section. An ancient settlement, Nicosia was made the administrative capital of Cyprus in around 965 CE by the Byzantine rulers of the island, but it only rose to prominence under Lusignan rule during the twelfth to fifteenth centuries. The distinctive, circular wall of the city center, with its eleven bastions, dates from the time of Venetian rule, built between 1567 and 1570. The city contains many Greek churches and Muslim mosques, which is evidence of its variable history.

LIMASSOL is a busy trading and tourist center and the island's busiest port. It has a natural harbor and has been occupied by people since the Bronze Age. Limassol was a Byzantine settlement and later a center for the Crusades. The town did not expand into an important trading center until the late nineteenth century, when it came under British protection. After the 1974 invasion, the city doubled in size, taking in forty-five thousand Greek Cypriot refugees. Today it has a population of 182,600 and is the second-largest city on the island. Many tourists who visit Cyprus spend time on the Bay of Amathus, just east of the town, where a 6-mile (10 km) stretch of hotels and man-made

Limassol is a popular vacation resort as well as a thriving port town.

The ancient ruins at Paphos mean the town now has **UNESCO** World Heritage site status.

beaches joins the town to the three-thousand-year-old ruins of Amathus. This, combined with visitors from the nearby British army base, ensures that Limassol has a lively nightlife and cosmopolitan atmosphere.

LARNACA Farther east along the southern coast is Larnaca, Cyprus's third-largest town. Larnaca, which has a regional population of 144,200 and an urban population of 85,700, reached its peak in the nineteenth century, when many international trading offices and consulates were based there for convenience. Since 1974, Larnaca has been the site of the island's international airport. To the east of Larnaca, the land is cramped, a consequence of the Turkish invasion and a demarcation line just to the north of the city. United Nations troops, Greek soldiers, and the many tourists who flock to this city give Larnaca an overcrowded appearance.

PAPHOS Situated on the southwest coast of the island, Paphos is a city with a truly glorious past. In ancient times, the settlement was a place of pilgrimage throughout the Hellenic world as a center for fertility rituals. Later, the small port became a Roman settlement. Paphos used to be a backward, undeveloped, sparsely populated area. However, this changed in 1982 when an airport was built to develop tourism. A new airport terminal opened in November 2008 adjacent to the old one. Now the city has a population of 64,400 and is increasingly popular with tourists. In 2017, it was named a European City of Culture by the European Union. Its ancient remains have earned the city a place on the United Nations Educational, Scientific, and Cultural Organization (UNESCO) list of cultural world heritage treasures.

FAMAGUSTA In the Turkish north, there are only two towns of significant size, Famagusta and Kyrenia. Founded by Ptolemy II in the third century BCE, Famagusta later fell to Arab conquerors, then became a Byzantine conquest in the twelfth century. During the Crusades, the town was a thriving center of

East-West trade. Following the Ottoman conquest in 1570, no Christian subject was allowed to live within its walls. The new town of Varosha was established nearby for Christians who had been expelled from Famagusta. Before the Turkish invasion in 1974, Varosha was a tourist town. Today, however, it is a ghost town. Famagusta, like Limassol, has a natural harbor—the deepest in all of Cyprus. But since the Turkish invasion in 1974, it is seldom used. Today, Famagusta has a population of around 40,900.

KYRENIA Located on the northern coast, Kyrenia was once known as the "jewel of the Levant" because of its picturesque setting and cosmopolitan social life. Following the 1974 invasion, many Anatolian Turks from the mainland settled here. Today, Kyrenia is a tranquil coastal town with a population of 20,800. Most of Kyrenia dates from the medieval and Ottoman periods. It boasts of a beautiful harbor, a medieval castle, and a promenade with Venetian-style facades.

INTERNET LINKS

https://apnews.com/9fd4f4273bad48cf8463c56872d14e2a
This news story describes how green and loggerhead turtles, which have laid their eggs on the beaches of Cyprus for thousands of years, are responding to conservation efforts. Although recently considered endangered, numbers for both species are increasing again.

http://www.moa.gov.cy/moa/ms/ms.nsf/DMLcyclimate_en/ DMLcyclimate_en?OpenDocument
This report from the Cyprus Department of Meteorology offers a detailed look at the climate of the island.

https://rainforests.mongabay.com/deforestation/archive/Cyprus.htm
Environmental and conservation publication *Mongabay* provides a detailed report on the status of forests in Cyprus, with statistics showing logging, growth of new forests, type of forest, and more.

HISTORY

The ancient mosaics at Curium are some of the finest of their kind anywhere in the world.

2

According to Greek legend, the goddess Aphrodite was born on Cyprus, and the island was the playground of the gods.

CYPRUS'S LOCATION AS A BRIDGE between Mediterranean Europe and the Middle East has made it the scene of many power struggles through thousands of years of history. Many nations and empires have fought to gain control of it as a means of accessing other territories. This means that the nation has often been a site of war, conflict, and occupation. On the other hand, Cyprus's location has made it a nation rich in ethnic diversity and culture.

ANCIENT CYPRUS

Evidence of human habitation in Cyprus dates from the Neolithic period, before 6000 BCE. Excavations at Khirokitia suggest that there was a settlement of about two thousand people, living in round stone houses. The community died out after a few centuries, and the island was uninhabited for two thousand years. The next period of habitation, the Sotira culture, dates from 4500 BCE. The people lived by hunting and fishing. In the Copper Age (3000—2500 BCE), people made tools and pots from copper.

During the late Bronze Age (1600—1200 BCE), Cyprus became absorbed into the Hittite Empire, and the island's contacts extended from the Aegean Sea to the Nile Delta. Mass immigration of Greek-speaking people from the Peloponnese occurred in the Iron Age (1100—700 BCE), establishing the Greek language and six kingdoms on the island: Curium, Paphos, Marion, Soli, Lapithos, and Salamis. Around 800 BCE, a new Phoenician colony was established at Citium. This culture had a great influence on Cyprus.

In 709 BCE, the kingdoms of Cyprus submitted to Assyrian rule. Assyrian domination ended in 669 BCE, and after that, Cyprus enjoyed a century of independence and exuberant artistic development. Later, Egypt became dominant in the eastern Mediterranean, and in 569 BCE, the Cypriot kings were forced to recognize the pharaoh Ahmose II as their ruler.

In 545 BCE, Cyprus was conquered by the Persians. The Persian expansion dragged Cyprus into a long war between the Greeks and the Persians. When the Ionians (a Greek people) revolted against Persian rule in 499 BCE, all the Cypriot kingdoms, except Amathus, joined the revolt. The revolt was suppressed after a year.

Greece and Persia continued to struggle for power in Cyprus. The island became an extremely important naval base in the eastern Mediterranean, and it was valued for its supplies of wood for shipbuilding. King Evagoras I of Salamis succeeded in unifying the island under his rule, but he was assassinated in 374 BCE.

After the swift conquest of the eastern Mediterranean by the Macedonian ruler Alexander the Great (356—323 BCE), Cyprus willingly became part of his vast empire. After his death in 323 BCE, the island kingdoms fell into the hands of Ptolemy I of Egypt in 294 BCE, and the island was held by Egypt for the next 250 years.

In 58 BCE, Cyprus was annexed by the expanding Roman republic. For the next six hundred years, Cyprus enjoyed the peace and stability brought about by integration into the Roman, and later Byzantine, Empire. The island's road network improved, and many public buildings were erected. The Roman garrison remained minimal, and Cypriots went about their affairs with little interference.

BYZANTIUM

When the Roman Empire divided in 395 CE, Cyprus remained a part of the Byzantine Empire. As Arabs of the Umayyad dynasty, under the leadership of Muawiya, swept through the eastern Mediterranean in the seventh century, they conquered the island in 649. In 688, a treaty between the Byzantine emperor Justinian II and the Arab ruler Abd al-Malik ibn Marwan effectively freed Cyprus from direct Arab rule for three hundred years, introducing an unstable period during which the island was forced to pay tribute to one or the other power, and sometimes both. Cyprus underwent great social changes during this time. There was an influx of Muslims and Arabs, and the island was constantly invaded by Arab forces and harassed by pirates. Many of the cities lay in permanent ruin. However, in 965, the Byzantine emperor Nicephorus II Phocas regained the island, and a period of economic and cultural prosperity followed.

Cyprus is the site of many well-preserved pieces of historic artwork. This mosaic shows the Virgin Mary and the baby Jesus.

THE LUSIGNAN DYNASTY

In 1185, the Byzantine governor of Cyprus, Isaac Comnenus, rebelled against Byzantium and declared himself emperor. However, he was defeated by King Richard I of England, who was on his way to the Holy Land during the Third Crusade. Richard later sold the island to Guy of Lusignan, the Crusader king who had lost Jerusalem to the forces of Saladin, the sultan of Egypt, following the Crusader defeat at the Battle of Hattin in 1187.

The Lusignan dynasty (1192—1489) ruled the island for the next three hundred years, although economic competition led Venice and Genoa to get involved in Cypriot affairs. During the reign of Peter II (1369—1382), both Genoa and Venice competed to control the island's valuable trade. Genoese troops seized Famagusta in 1374 and held it for the next ninety years. The last Lusignan king, Jacques II (reigned 1460 to 1473), regained the throne and managed to expel the Genoese from Famagusta. His wife, Caterina Cornaro, succeeded him, but she ceded Cyprus to Venice during her reign (1474—1489). Venice controlled Cyprus for eighty-two years.

During the Lusignan period, Famagusta was one of the richest cities in the known world, yet today it is called the "ghost city."

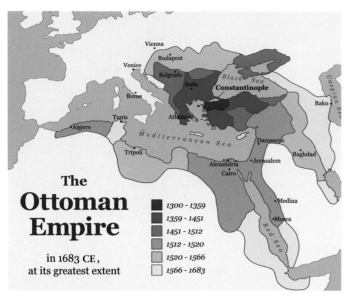

The Ottoman Empire

in 1683 CE,
at its greatest extent

- 1300 - 1359
- 1359 - 1451
- 1451 - 1512
- 1512 - 1520
- 1520 - 1566
- 1566 - 1683

At its peak, the Ottoman Empire extended through much of the Mediterranean region and North Africa.

PART OF AN EMPIRE

From the base of their power in the old Byzantine heartland in Turkey, the Ottomans grew in power during the sixteenth century, capturing Syria, Palestine, and Egypt. In 1570, 350 Turkish ships landed at Larnaca, and Cyprus fell to the Ottomans the next year. Twenty thousand Turks settled on the island after the conquest, while most of the Latin inhabitants emigrated. For the next three hundred years, Cyprus became a poor, undeveloped backwater of the Ottoman Empire.

One of the most significant consequences of Ottoman rule was a steady increase in the Turkish population. Turks made up 31 percent of the island's population by 1841. However, there was little mixing between Turks and Greeks, partly because of their different status under Ottoman rule, but mainly because of religious differences. A second significant development was the gradual increase in the power of the Orthodox Church. Under the Ottomans, religious leaders were assumed to have political power and responsibilities, making the Orthodox Church more and more powerful in the Greek community.

Nevertheless, abuses of power and corruption were common. High taxes were levied in an arbitrary manner on both Greek and Turkish peasants. The rural population grew increasingly dissatisfied with their lot under the thumb of both Turkish rulers and wealthy Orthodox clergy. When the Greek nationalist uprising against the Ottoman Empire occurred on the Greek mainland in 1821, a backlash against Greek Cypriots resulted in massacres of local intellectuals and clergymen. Troops were brought in from Syria and Egypt, and a six-month reign of terror left many dead. This caused resentment among the Greeks and an increase in the nationalist feelings the massacres were intended to quell. Turkish envy rose because of Greek prosperity and higher levels of education. Many poorer rural Turks had become second-class citizens in a country they had conquered only a few hundred years before.

BRITISH RULE

The Greek war of liberation marked the beginning of the swift decline of the Ottoman Empire. British power extended through the eastern Mediterranean in the nineteenth century. Turkey's weakening power and the opening of the Suez Canal in 1869 gave the British more and more influence over the Turkish authorities. The Cyprus Convention of 1878 said that Britain would administer the island, which would remain under Turkish sovereignty. The agreement was seen as part of a deal in which the British would reinforce Turkish power against the increasing threat of Russian expansion in the Caucasus on Turkey's northern border. Britain wanted to make sure its trade route through the Suez Canal to India would be protected.

With the start of World War I and a declaration of hostilities between Turkey and Britain in 1914, Britain annexed the island. The island officially became a British colony in 1925. British rule brought increasing efficiency to the outmoded and corrupt administration of Cyprus. A modern education system was introduced, with separate schools for Christians and Muslims. Contact with Western Europe meant that Cypriot trade boomed for the first time in more than three hundred years. A legislative council was formed, consisting of both Cypriots and the British, for making joint administrative decisions. However, British modernization only affected the cities; little change occurred in the villages. Taxes were high under British rule, and Britain invested little in developing the island's infrastructure.

Disillusionment with British rule and an increase in Greek nationalism led Greek Cypriots to demand to be united with the Greek motherland. Such demands led to riots in Nicosia in 1931. During World War II, Cyprus was not directly involved in the fighting, and the island gained from a boom in the economy.

CLOSER RELATIONS WITH GREECE?

The end of World War II increased Greek Cypriot calls for enosis, or union with Greece. Fearing marginalization, the Turkish minority, which made up about 20 percent of the population, was hostile to this demand. Likewise, Turkey viewed the development of a potentially hostile state to its immediate south with some alarm. Britain was eager to hold on to Cyprus as part of the military presence of NATO (North Atlantic Treaty Organization) in the Middle East, and so discouraged enosis. In 1955, Greek guerrilla groups stepped up in actions against the British, who were increasingly viewed as an occupation force. The National Organization for Cypriot Struggle (Ethniki Orgánosis Kipriakoú Agónos, or EOKA) bombed military buildings and attacked opponents of enosis, killing both British officers and Cypriots. Turkish Cypriots formed their own terror units, campaigning for *taksim* (tahk-SIHM), or division of the island. The British government drew up proposals for self-government, but the Greeks continued to pursue their nationalist aspirations. The two Cypriot communities became more polarized, and communal violence escalated into civil war in 1958.

Under pressure from the United States, the Greek and Turkish governments came to an agreement in 1959 that was accepted by the British government and leaders of the Greek and Turkish Cypriot communities. Cyprus became an independent republic on August 16, 1960. The agreement stated that Cyprus would not unite with any other state or be subject to partition. Britain agreed to guarantee the island's sovereignty and military security in exchange for maintaining two military bases on the island. To prevent minority discrimination, Turks and Greeks were represented separately in the parliament, administration, police, and army.

THE MOVE TO INDEPENDENCE

The first independent elections were held in 1960, resulting in supporters of Archbishop Makarios III, a prominent advocate for enosis during the 1950s, winning thirty out of the thirty-five Greek Cypriot parliamentary seats, while Dr. Fazil Küçük and his supporters won all fifteen Turkish Cypriot seats. Makarios became Cyprus's first president, with Küçük as his deputy. In 1963, political disagreement arose, and fighting broke out between the two communities. Nicosia was divided—as it is today—by a ceasefire line, called the "green line." Turkish Cypriots were reduced to living in a few urban enclaves and became reliant on relief packages for food and other essentials.

Nicosia is currently the only capital city in the world divided between two countries. The United Nations (UN) buffer zone, or "green line," runs through it and contains a "no-man's-land" where no one is allowed except for a few military forces. Within this no-man's-land lie dozens of abandoned buildings, including the former Nicosia airport. While everyday life continues in both Turkish and Greek Cyprus, in this buffer zone, everything is as it was forty years ago.

The situation increased tensions between Turkey and Greece. By 1964, the United Nations had agreed to send a multinational peacekeeping force to replace British peacekeeping efforts. However, fighting intensified, and Turkish military aircraft intervened in some actions. Both Greece and Turkey began secretly sending regular troops to train and reinforce the warring factions.

In 1967, violence between Greek and Turkish Cypriots led to Turkish threats to invade. The Greek military junta of the time agreed to withdraw their regular troops, and an uneasy peace was established. Turkish Cypriots were allowed to leave their enclaves and live and work where they pleased. Makarios was reelected president in 1968 and again in 1973. The Greek junta's relations with Makarios worsened because he was thought to have become content with Cypriot independence, while many Greek Cypriots still wanted union with the mainland. A struggle for power within the Greek nationalist community ensued.

A NATION DIVIDED

On July 15, 1974, mainland Greek military officers who supported the nationalist cause led a violent coup against Makarios and his republican supporters. Many left-wingers and republicans were murdered, and the presidential palace was left in ruins. The long-awaited enosis had been achieved overnight. Most of the population, both Greek and Turkish, looked on helplessly, while Makarios escaped to the safety of the British military base at Akrotiri. Nikos Sampson, a right-wing radical, was proclaimed president. However, Turkey would not tolerate the establishment of an overtly nationalist government that would

United Nations Peacekeepers patrol the buffer zone that divides north and south Cyprus.

potentially threaten its southern coast. Five days after the coup, Turkish troops landed on the northern beaches of Cyprus, establishing a base around Kyrenia that linked to the Turkish sector of Nicosia. Vigorous fighting ensued.

Events in Greece created further confusion, with the fallen junta being replaced by a democratic government under Konstantinos Karamanlis on July 23. However, agreement was not reached among the guarantor powers, Greece, Britain, and Turkey, until August 16, by which time the Turkish army controlled 37 percent of the island. As many as 165,000 Greeks fled the northern part of the island, leaving their possessions and property behind. Many lived in hastily built camps in southern Cyprus for months. Around 51,000 Turkish Cypriots were thought to have fled to the north to escape the bloody reprisals of Greek nationalists.

In 1983, the Turkish part of the island declared itself an independent state, the Turkish Republic of Northern Cyprus (TRNC). However, except for its ally and sponsor Turkey, no countries in the world recognize its legal independence today. UN-sponsored talks took place in 1992, 1995, and 1999 to try to come to a lasting settlement, but there was little real progress. In 2003, glimmers of hope arose when people crossed the border between north and south freely for the first time in thirty years. Although this showed progress on both sides, and gave people the opportunity to have jobs and participate in leisure activities in either nation, talks of reunification continued to be unsuccessful. A referendum in 2004 resulted in the desire to continue separation. Thus, a divided Cyprus joined the European Union (EU) in 2004, along with nine other new members from Central and Eastern Europe. The division of Cyprus has remained a source of conflict that has soured relations between Turkey and Greece, which are both members of the NATO alliance, and has also stalled Turkey's proposed membership in the EU.

In 2012, the United Nations canceled a reunification conference, claiming that neither side showed any interest in making progress. Talks resumed the following year, but they stopped temporarily in 2014 when Turkey sent ships to start drilling for gas in territory that remains contested. The gas fields have remained a source of tension, with both sides claiming ownership and the right to drill. Repeated peace talks failed to bring about a solution as of 2018.

As of 2018, the president of Cyprus was Nicos Anastasiades. He was elected to a second term in February 2018

BASES IN CYPRUS

Today, there are still British troops based at Akrotiri and Dhekelia, most of them working in intelligence and surveillance for the British and US military. In recent years, the Cypriot government has demanded the return of the land and the closure of the bases. In July 2001, locals protested at the bases, angry over British plans to construct radio masts as part of an upgrade of British military communication posts. They argued that this would damage the environment and increase the risk of cancer to local residents. The British showed no intention of giving up the bases, although they offered to surrender 45 square miles (117 sq km) of farmland as part of a UN-brokered peace plan. This would equal half of the land area held by the British but would still leave them with enough land for military purposes. In 2017, the British government reiterated its intent to return half of its territory if both the Turkish and Greek sides of the island could come to an agreement. However, no agreement was immediately forthcoming.

INTERNET LINKS

https://www.bbc.co.uk/news/world-europe-17219505
This BBC timeline offers a breakdown of key events in Cypriot history throughout the twentieth century and to the present day. .

https://www.globalsecurity.org/military/library/report/2004/annan-cyprus-problem_maps_26feb03.pdf
The full text of the proposed Annan Plan details joint plans by Turkish and Greek Cypriot leaders to resolve "the Cyprus problem" and seek reunification.

http://www.whatson-northcyprus.com/history/ottoman.htm
This brief history of the Ottoman period in Cyprus outlines key events and figures from 1571 to 1878.

GOVERNMENT

ΠΑΡΘΕΝΑΓΩΓΕΙΟΝ ΦΑΝΕΡΩΜΕΝΗΣ

This government building sits in Nicosia's downtown area.

OFFICIALLY, THE GOVERNMENT OF the Republic of Cyprus in the Greek-dominated south is in charge. However, in the north the Turkish majority claims to be independent of republic rule. Internationally, only the republic is recognized as a legitimate government.

A DIVIDED GOVERNMENT

After Cypriot independence from British rule in 1960, a new constitution was drafted. It determined that a Greek president and a Turkish vice president each be elected for terms of five years. Today, all citizens, regardless of ethnic origin, have the right to vote for both positions. The government also consists of a House of Representatives. This is made up of eighty voting seats (originally fifty, but the number was changed in 1984). Of these, fifty-six are for Greek Cypriots and twenty-four for Turkish Cypriots; however, the Turkish seats have not been filled since the beginning of the ethnic conflict. An additional three nonvoting seats are assigned to the Maronite, Armenian, and Roman Catholic communities. Each representative is elected for a five-year term.

After ratification in 1960, the constitution faced opposition almost immediately, particularly since it divided government rule along ethnic lines. In 1963, it was partly suspended. Since then, the constitution has been amended several times, as recently as 2016.

THE REPUBLIC GOVERNMENT

As the official government of the island, the Republic of Cyprus still enforces the constitution of 1960. However, since the withdrawal of Turkish Cypriot participation in government in 1964, the joint provisions in the constitution have been altered to ensure a noncommunal, single-representative government and administration. The president represents the republic at all official functions. A council of ministers holds executive power, controlling public services, monetary policy, foreign policy, and the drafting and passing of laws. Council members are appointed by the president.

Local government in the republic is at district, municipal, and village levels. The government appoints district officers, while local councils and municipal mayors are elected.

Stavros Malas (*center*) campaigns during the 2018 presidential election. He lost to incumbent Nicos Anastasiades.

PARTIES IN GOVERNMENT

The oldest established party in the Republic of Cyprus is the communist AKEL, or Progressive Party of the Working People, founded in 1941. A pro-Soviet party, the AKEL achieved much success during the first twenty-five years of the republic, averaging 30 percent of the vote. Despite the breakup of the Soviet Union, the party remains powerful in Greek Cypriot politics. The AKEL campaigns for a demilitarized, nonaligned, and independent Cyprus. AKEL is currently the main opposition party, holding sixteen seats. The current majority party, the DISY, or Democratic Rally Party, seeks greater integration for Cyprus with Europe, especially through membership in the European Union. They currently hold eighteen seats. Other parties with seats in the current House of Representatives include the DIKO, or Democratic Party (9); the KS-EDEK, or Socialist Party of Cyprus (3); the SYPOL, or Citizens' Alliance (3); the KA, or Solidarity Movement (3); the KOSP, or Movement of Ecologists (2); and the ELAM, or National Popular Front (2).

Cyprus has a very low crime rate and is considered one of the safest destinations in Europe.

In the 2016 legislative election, while the majority of votes (56 percent) went to parties that made seeking reunification with the north a priority, some political experts said that the low voter turnout may indicate frustration with ongoing talks.

In 2018, the people of Cyprus headed to the polls to elect a president. The election began with a total of nine contenders, all male. Typically, there are two rounds of voting in the presidential vote. If no contender wins more than 50 percent of the votes cast in the first round, the top two candidates proceed to a second round. The winner of that round takes the office of president for the next five years.

In January, incumbent president Nicos Anastasiades of the DISY came in first with 35.5 percent of the vote. AKEL candidate Stavros Malas came in second with 30 percent. In February's second-round run-off, Anastasiades won with 56 percent of the vote, thus earning a second term as president.

Voter turnout for the election was low as many Cypriots called the candidates uninspiring or untrustworthy. Major issues during the election period were reunification, financial security, and worries about corruption in government.

THE LEGAL SYSTEM

The legal codes of the republic are based on a combination of Roman law and English common law. The republic has a separate police force and legal administration. The government appoints the judges, but the judiciary is entirely independent of executive power. Courts exist at the supreme and district levels. District and assize courts deal with civil and criminal cases, while the Supreme Court is the final court of appeal for cases from district courts and adjudication in constitutional and administrative law.

The Supreme Court, located in Nicosia, consists of thirteen judges, each appointed by the president. The four district courts are located in Nicosia, Larnaca, Limassol, and Paphos. District courts have both civil and criminal divisions, but judges may only sentence a person up to five years in prison. More serious cases are dealt with in an assize court, where a panel of three judges presides.

In February 2018, Nicos Anastasiades was elected to a second term as president of the Republic of Cyprus. Anastasiades was born in 1946 in Pera Pedi and trained as a lawyer, graduating from the University of Athens and then from University College London, having completed graduate studies in shipping law.

He was first elected to the Cyprus House of Representatives in 1981. From 1997 on, he served as leader of the Democratic Rally. In 2012, he was nominated as his party's candidate in the 2013 Cyprus presidential election. One of the key parts of his campaign was a promise to reduce the length of military conscription from twenty-four months to fourteen months. Military service is compulsory for all Cypriot males, but Anastasiades argued that the longer term created economic hardship for some families. After becoming Cyprus's seventh president in February 2013, he did indeed work to reduce the conscription length to fourteen months.

In February 2018, he was elected to a second term as president. Much of his campaign focused on his success in leading Cyprus out of economic recession. After reelection, he also promised to resume reunification talks, saying, "The biggest challenge we face is reunifying our country. I will continue to work with the same determination in a bid to achieve our common goal—ending foreign occupation and reunifying our state. There are no winners or losers, just Cyprus." Reunification is an issue that Anastasiades has supported since the United Nations launched the Annan Plan for reunification between northern Cyprus and the republic in 2004. Back then, Anastasiades's advocacy was controversial since more than 60 percent of his own party opposed the plan. Fourteen years later, the issue is still important to him.

THE NORTHERN GOVERNMENT

A provisional body, the Turkish Cypriot Federated State (1975—1983), was established to govern Turkish Cyprus soon after the Turkish invasion. Following a stalemate in negotiations, the Turkish Republic of North Cyprus (TRNC) was declared in 1983, and the people approved a new constitution in a referendum in 1985. However, only Turkey recognizes the self-proclaimed state, and no other countries have direct communication links or diplomatic relations with North Cyprus. The TRNC relies on Turkey for much of its international sea and air links and trade. It also ensures that Turkey is a powerful player in TRNC politics.

The TRNC is a secular republic governed by a unicameral Legislative Assembly of fifty deputies. These deputies are elected every five years. The country is run by a council of ten ministers appointed by the president, on the advice of the prime minister, who is chosen from among the Legislative Assembly.

The north held its first multiparty parliamentary elections in 1993, removing the long-ruling National Unity Party in favor of a coalition of the Democratic Party (DP) and Republican Turkish Party (CTP). In 1996, a new coalition was formed between the two main right-wing, nationalist parties, the National Unity Party (UBP) and the Democratic Party, which held power for the next eight years. In 2003, the CTP and DP formed a new government, with CTP leader Mehmet Ali Talat becoming the new prime minister. In 2005, CTP deputy leader Ferdi Sabit Soyer took over as prime minister after Talat's election as president the same year. Talat served until 2010, when Derviş Eroğlu replaced him. In 2015, Mustafa Akinci became president.

Mustafa Akinci became president of northern Cyprus in 2015.

In legislative elections in April 2009, the anti-unification UBP won power in northern Cyprus, gaining twenty-six seats in the fifty-seat parliament, with 44 percent of the vote. Although the UBP is against unification with Greek-dominated southern Cyprus, it wants talks to continue for the sake of achieving a two-state solution. The UBP retained twenty-one seats in the most recent election in 2018. The pro-reunification Republican Turkish Party (CTP) holds twelve seats. Other seats are held by the People's Party (9), the Communal Democracy Party (3), the Democratic Party (3), and the Rebirth Party (2).

Presidential elections take place every five years. A candidate has to win at least 50 percent of the votes—an absolute majority—to secure an outright victory. Otherwise, the two candidates who receive the most votes go to second-round voting one week later, and the winner becomes the president.

From 1975 to 2005, the president of the Turkish Republic of Northern Cyprus was Rauf Denktaş. A committed nationalist, he tried to gain international recognition for the TRNC. However, his approach proved to be a major barrier to reconciliation with southern Cyprus and tended to polarize opinion on both sides of the divided island. In 2005, Rauf Denktaş retired from the presidency. Mehmet Ali Talat, the sitting prime minister, won the presidential election, becoming the TRNC's second president. The most recent elections were held in 2015. In the first round, incumbent president Derviş Eroğlu won 28.2 percent of the vote, closely followed by Mustafa Akinci, who won 26.9 percent of the vote. Both candidates progressed to the second round. Akinci won in a surprise upset, with 60.5 percent of the vote. In April 2015, Mustafa Akinci became the fourth president of the TRNC. He ran as a leftist moderate who promised to "push harder for a peace deal" and to end discrimination against women and LGBT citizens.

BRIDGING THE DIVIDE

Discussions between Greek and Turkish Cypriots were an ongoing part of the Cypriot political scene even before independence. Since the Turkish invasion, negotiators from both sides of the ethnic divide have met on many occasions in the hope of finding a solution to their differences. UN mediators have produced a plan in which Cyprus becomes an independent republic—with two zones—a proposal that both sides have broadly accepted in principle.

Nevertheless, over the years, negotiations have faced some stumbling blocks. The distribution of power between the two communities remains unclear. The Greek Cypriots campaign for a powerful central authority, which they would probably control by virtue of their numbers. Turkish Cypriots seek greater power for local districts, which would give them more autonomy. The Greeks seek freedom of movement within the whole federation, so Greek Cypriots would be able to return to their homes and land in the north. Turkish Cypriots, however, reject this plan, fearing that they might quickly become a minority in their own sector. The Greek Cypriots demand the withdrawal of Turkish troops from the island. The Turkish Cypriots, on the other hand, want a Turkish military presence to ensure their security and political rights. The presidency is also a contentious point. Although both sides agree that there

ANNAN PLAN

Also known as the Cyprus Reunification Plan, the Annan Plan was devised by the United Nations in 2002 as a means to resolve the situation in Cyprus. After a series of meetings with both Turkish Cypriot and Greek Cypriot leaders, it was proposed that a United Republic of Cyprus be created. It would be a federation of the two states joined under a common government. It was based partly on the model of Swiss government and would have a presidential council, an evenly split senate, a proportionally divided lower chamber, and a Supreme Court comprising three Greek Cypriot judges, three Turkish Cypriot judges, and three foreign justices.

The United Republic of Cyprus would have a new flag, a new constitution, and a new national anthem. A reconciliation commission would also be created to help resolve any disputes and to reunite the two communities.

A referendum was held in April 2004 to vote on the Annan Plan. Although it was supported by the majority of Turks, the majority of Greeks were against the plan. Many said their biggest concern was security, since a Turkish military would be established.

Experts later said that the Annan Plan was flawed from the very beginning. All negotiations were held behind closed doors between politicians and then presented for a vote. The Cypriot people had very little input.

should be rotating Greek and Turkish presidents, this may prove difficult to carry out in practice.

A hint of promise seemed to materialize in 2002 when the Annan Plan was created. However, since the referendum that followed in 2004 did not have a favorable result, hope for reunification quickly diminished. This outcome led to other divisions soon after.

Because both sides needed to approve the Annan Plan, the island remained divided when Cyprus was officially admitted into the EU in May 2004. Although the whole of the island is considered legally part of the Republic of Cyprus, only southern Cyprus, which is under the direct control of the internationally recognized government, enjoys the benefits of EU membership.

UN secretary general Kofi Annan (*right*) meets then Cyprus president Tassos Papadopoulos (*left*) in 2004.

Presidents Akinci (*left*) and Anastasiades (*right*) have had an often rocky relationship but gave a surprise joint address to the nation in December 2015.

Further talks were held between leaders of the two communities in 2006, and again in 2008, after the election of Dimitris Christofias as Cypriot president in February of that year. Christofias had very good relations with Turkish Cypriot president Mehmet Ali Talat, and many Cypriots were optimistic that a power-sharing agreement could be reached. Travel restrictions were lifted and border crossings were opened in the divided capital of Nicosia. However, the talks stalled, and the victory of the anti-unification National Unity Party (UBP) in elections in northern Cyprus in April 2009 made a quick resolution less likely.

Turkey also wants the situation to be resolved: Turkey's plans to join the EU are linked to a peaceful outcome of the Cyprus question. After Turkish Cypriots supported the UN-backed plan for power sharing in the failed 2004 referendum, the EU pledged to introduce policies to end northern Cyprus's international isolation and began giving economic aid to the country. Despite ongoing talks, negotiations for Turkey to join the EU appear to have stopped by 2017, with the EU citing human rights issues as a barrier for membership.

Reunification is still the subject of frequent talks, and Presidents Anastasiades and Akinci have both expressed a desire for a peaceful settlement. In December 2015, they gave a surprise joint television address to wish the nation a happy holiday period. Their original plan to reach a settlement in 2016 did not come to fruition, but after the reelection of Anastasiades in 2018, it was announced that talks would resume. However, Akinci has sometimes expressed frustration with the Greek Cypriot government, saying that they are "all talk and no action."

http://www.cyprusprofile.com/en/country-information/politics
This article outlines the government and political system in Cyprus. It includes a list of current political parties and their leaders, and current government ministers.

https://www.dw.com/en/cyprus-president-nicos-anastasiades -re-elected/a-42438533
Cyprus president Nicos Anastasiades was reelected in 2018. This news story covers the election campaign and the final vote.

http://www.nsd.uib.no/european_election_database/country/ cyprus/parties.html
This detailed breakdown of Cyprus's political parties explains their history, key campaign positions, and numbers of votes and seats in each recent election.

https://www.politico.eu/article/cyprus-reunification-two-votes -one-last-chance
This article explores the recent presidential elections in both southern and northern Cyprus, and explains what the elections might mean for hopes of future reunification.

http://www.studiofinpro.it/wp-content/uploads/INTRODUCTION -TO-CYPRUS-LEGAL-SYSTEM.pdf
This introduction to the Cyprus legal system provides an easy-to-understand explanation of each type of court and what they do, as well as offering a history of the island's legal system and how it developed during the time of British colonization.

ECONOMY

The currencies of both regions of Cyprus are pictured here. There are Turkish lira and Euros mixed together.

The currency in the Republic of Cyprus is the euro. Northern Cyprus uses the Turkish lira.

THE REPUBLIC OF CYPRUS HAS repeatedly gained recognition as one of the fastest-growing economies in the European Union. That is no small feat, given its small island status and the setbacks it faced in the recent global recession. The country's service-based economy thrived in the late twentieth century and the first part of the twenty-first century. Over the past few decades, there has been a noticeable shift from an agriculture-based economy to tourism, finance, and real estate.

Despite the International Monetary Fund's ranking of Cyprus as one of the most advanced economies in the world, it has faced one major weakness. Being so closely linked to neighboring EU economies, particularly that of Greece, made it especially vulnerable during the financial collapse of 2010.

In addition to a certain amount of financial dependence on neighbors— southern Cyprus to Greece and northern Cyprus to Turkey—the island is reliant upon trade since it has so few natural resources. Industrial equipment, fuel, and many daily food resources must be imported. Nevertheless, Cyprus has also developed a strong export market for some foods, building supplies, and fabrics.

THE ECONOMY OF THE SOUTHERN REPUBLIC

Agriculture's contribution to the Cypriot economy is shrinking, but it remains an important part of island life.

Between 1960 and 1974, before partition, Cyprus operated a successful, free-enterprise economy based on trade and agriculture that was the envy of its neighbors. Since 1974, the south has created an economic miracle. The economy of the Republic of Cyprus is dominated by the service sector—tourism, property development, and financial services—making up 86.8 percent of the country's GDP. Tourism is one of the most important sectors of the economy, followed by financial services and real estate. The country's dependence on tourism means that economic conditions in the rest of Europe have a huge influence on the island's prosperity. Because it is dependent on foreign revenue, the economy is vulnerable to changes in the economies of Europe and the Middle East. Still, the standard of living in the republic is higher than that in any of its eastern Mediterranean neighbors.

Main export partners are Libya (9.4 percent), Greece (7.7 percent), Norway (6.7 percent), the United Kingdom (5.3 percent), and Germany (4.1 percent). The island's biggest partners for imports are Greece (19 percent), Italy (7.5 percent), and China (7.4 percent). Leading exports are citrus fruit, potatoes, pharmaceuticals, cement, and clothing.

Cyprus imports most of its consumer goods, petroleum, machinery, and transportation equipment. Prior to the recession that hit in 2009, unemployment rates in Cyprus hovered around 4 percent. This increased significantly but is once again showing signs of improving. The 2017 unemployment rate was 11.8 percent, an improvement on the previous year's rate of 13 percent. Approximately 30 percent of young people between the ages of fifteen and twenty-four are unemployed. Full-time employees work roughly 40 hours a week, while part-time workers work 21.5 hours.

Small farms were the backbone of the Cypriot economy when the country gained independence in 1960. Large-scale irrigation projects meant that crops, especially fruit and vegetables, could be exported to Western Europe. Following the Turkish invasion of the north, agriculture became unevenly distributed on the divided island. Citrus fruits, cereal crops, and tobacco remained in the Turkish zone, but most of the grape crop was located in the south. In 1978, 23 percent of the working population in the south was employed in agriculture.

BANKING CRISIS IN GREECE

Cyprus's close ties with Greece have often proved to be a benefit to the small Mediterranean island. However, those ties recently proved to be an economic burden when Greece's banks collapsed.

Banking and finance make up a significant portion of the service sector contribution to Cyprus's GDP. Cyprus joined the EU in 2004 and adopted the euro as its form of currency in January 2008. During Cyprus's first few years of EU membership, its economy continued to thrive. However, in 2009, the nation entered a recession. The situation was not unique to Cyprus or to Europe. Banks around the world were in a state of financial crisis. By 2010, Greek banks were failing. Since the two major banks in Cyprus had large holdings tied up in the Greek markets, they too suffered. In summer 2012, the Cypriot government requested economic support from the European Union.

Nicos Anastasiades was elected president in February 2013, and shortly afterward, he negotiated a bailout agreement. As part of the deal, banks closed for two weeks and there were two years of strict economic controls. Cyprus's two biggest banks merged as part of the recovery effort.

In 2015, Cyprus emerged from the recession one year earlier than expected and received excellent ratings for its recovery. Although unemployment had risen during the previous few years, conditions have improved since then, and Cyprus's economy is showing signs of strong growth again.

However, since that time, the agricultural sector has shrunk, employing just 3.8 percent of the workforce in 2014 and providing just 2.3 percent of national GDP (2017 estimate).

Strangely for an island, Cyprus has only a small fishing industry and imports most of its fish and seafood. This is chiefly because of a shortage of plankton in the island's waters. Plankton are tiny organisms that fish feed on for nutrients. Small fishing boats go for sole, whitebait, and red mullet, while commercial vessels look for swordfish.

Industry, which includes manufacturing, mining, and construction, contributes 11 percent to the republic's GDP each year and employs 15.2 percent of the workforce. Natural resources are few, so industrial development is limited. The manufacturing industry produces piping and cement. Bricks, tiles, clothing, footwear, and wood and paper products are also made.

Tourism has been a major part of the economy of Cyprus since 1960. Following the Turkish invasion of northern Cyprus in 1974, Turkish forces occupied many tourist hotels and important cultural attractions. However, following partition, the tourist trade in the Greek-controlled south rapidly recovered, with many new tourist developments and luxury hotels springing up around Paphos in the west, Limassol in the south, and Larnaca and Ayia Napa in the east. Since the mid-1980s, tourism has been the largest source of foreign income for the Republic of Cyprus, making up 12 percent of GDP in 2016.

Between 1997 and 2008, every year between 2 million and 2.6 million people visited Cyprus. Income from tourism increased noticeably from 2002 through 2007 after Cyprus joined the EU. Tourist numbers remained steady in 2006 and 2007, with approximately 2.4 million tourist visits in both years, mostly vacationers from Northern and Western Europe. However, the world economic downturn hit the tourist industry in 2008 and 2009. In 2008, there was a small decrease in tourist arrivals from the previous year, with tourist earnings down by 3.5 percent. Figures at the beginning of 2009 showed tourist earnings to have dropped by as much as 12 percent, and arrivals were down by 15 percent as a result of the global recession. Tourist numbers quickly rebounded after the recession, with Cyprus welcoming a record-breaking 3.18 million visitors in 2016. Some economists believe the tourism sector could make up as much as 30 percent of the GDP by the year 2030.

THE NORTHERN ECONOMY

The north's diplomatic isolation from the international community has forced the TRNC to rely heavily on Turkey for external trade and investment. The country's economy and infrastructure have been integrated into that of the mainland, and the Turkish currency, the Turkish lira, is legal tender in the north. This means that the economy of Cyprus is very much linked to the well-being of Turkey. However, the benefit of this is that their dependence on Turkey, combined with a lack of a major financial sector market, kept them relatively stable while their neighbors to the south were weathering the recession. For years, Turkey has provided aid to nearly every sector of the TRNC economy, including tourism, industry, and education.

The economy relies heavily on agriculture and government services, which together employ more than half the workforce. As of 2012, the service sector made up 58.7 percent of the economy. Much of this is concentrated in state administration and trade, and less is dedicated to tourism, financial services, and real estate development.

The TRNC exports dairy products, citrus fruit, raki (an aniseed-flavored alcoholic drink), potatoes, and chicken to Turkey and the Middle East, and imports food, minerals, chemicals, and machinery. Most imported goods come from Turkey (64.7 percent) and the European Union (15.5 percent). The EU's role as an export partner has declined, now accounting for 6.2 percent of all exports, while the role of Middle Eastern nations as trading partners has dramatically increased. A low tariff barrier for Turkish goods and the superior development of the Turkish industry means that Turkish imports remain cheap and more competitive compared to local products. This, and the use of the Turkish lira, has led to high levels of inflation imported from the mainland. These factors have limited the growth of small-scale manufacturing in the TRNC.

Agriculture contributes 6.2 percent to the north's wealth each year. It employs 14.5 percent of the working population and is an essential foreign currency earner. Most of the island's crops are grown on the Mesaoria Plain, including olives, potatoes, wheat, barley, and tobacco. Guzelyurt, an area around Morphou, is the market garden of Cyprus, where oranges and other citrus fruit are grown in abundance. Fishing and growing tobacco are the main activities on the remote Karpas Peninsula. The main fishing ports are Bogaz and Kumyali. Animal farming primarily involves chickens, sheep, and goats.

Industry, including manufacturing and construction, contributes 35.1 percent to GDP. Most industrial output is absorbed by the domestic market. The growth of local industry has been hampered by difficulties in reaching international markets, an inability to attract new investment, and the competition of cheap imports from Turkey. Citrus, dairy, potatoes, and textiles are the chief exports.

North Cyprus has a far less developed tourist industry than the south, but it has grown in popularity because of its reputation for unspoiled natural beauty. In 2012, more than one million tourists visited northern Cyprus. Most came from Turkey and the Arab world, but a large number came from the United Kingdom. Since the late 1970s, northern Cyprus has been advertised as a shopping destination for Turkish tourists. Most tourists still stay in hotels in and around the beaches of Kyrenia and Famagusta. Like its southern

The Bank of Cyprus is the largest bank on the island. Approximately 83 percent of Cypriots hold accounts there.

Potatoes are an important export crop for northern Cyprus.

counterpart, the north's tourism sector was affected by the recent economic downturn; fewer people were traveling. However, the industry shows strong signs of recovery.

GETTING AROUND

Northern and southern Cyprus are served by separate transportation systems, and there are no services linking the two parts of the island. The Republic of Cyprus has 8,082 miles (13,006 km) of road, while the TRNC has 4,350 miles (7,000 km) of road. Modern, four-lane highways link Nicosia with Larnaca and Limassol, and Limassol to Paphos. However, a substantial part of the road system in the rural and mountainous areas is still unpaved. An extensive bus service allows Cypriots in rural areas to travel to the main towns and cities. The roads in northern Cyprus are less developed than those in the south and are far less busy. Cypriots drive on the left side of the road. There has been no functioning railroad in Cyprus since 1952.

The main international seaports in the south are Limassol and Larnaca. They act as transshipment terminals for cargo going to and from the eastern Mediterranean. Today, Larnaca mainly functions as a berth for oil tankers.

In the north, Famagusta and Kyrenia still operate sea traffic with the Turkish mainland. Until the Turkish invasion, Famagusta was the island's most important seaport. Today, it only serves the Turkish region. Vehicle ferries operate between Famagusta and Mersin in southern Turkey, and during the summer season, passenger and car ferries also run to Kyrenia.

The republic's main international airport is near Larnaca. A smaller but busy airport has also been built at Paphos. At the height of the tourist season, dozens of flights come into these airports every day. The national carrier, Cyprus Airways, ceased operations in 2015, but another company has taken over the right to use the name. There are three registered air carriers based in Cyprus—the new Cyprus Airways, Cobalt Air, and Tus Airways. Turkish Cyprus's chief international link is Ercan, a small airport east of Nicosia. Only Turkish Airlines has regularly scheduled flights to Ercan. Chartered flights carrying tourists from Britain and other parts of Northern Europe fly to Ercan but have to touch down in Turkey first.

THE TOURIST DOLLAR

Tourism has been Cyprus's biggest and most important growth industry since the partition in 1983, with the southern part of the island now receiving more than two million visitors a year. Visitors swamp Cyprus from the summer to the autumn, outnumbering the local population. The beaches around Limassol, the resorts of Ayia Napa and Protaris at Cape Greco in the far southeastern corner, and the historical town of Paphos in the west offer numerous first-class hotels and tourist facilities for those seeking sun and sand.

Most of these resorts have been developed since the partition. Forest stations have been built to accommodate tourists in the Troodos Mountains, and numerous forest trails have been developed. The boom in the tourist industry has had positive consequences for the republic's construction industry, with the building of many hotels, apartments, and restaurants. Tourist centers such as Ayia Napa, for example, were insignificant rural villages some thirty years ago, but with the explosion of tourism, they have developed into a vast complex of hotels, restaurants, clubs, bars, and recreational facilities. The ancient sites of Curium, Citium, Amathus, Khirokitia, and Paphos are an added attraction.

INTERNET LINKS

http://www.cyprusprofile.com/en/economy
This article provides an economic overview of Cyprus, looking at the recent financial downturn and how the nation has recovered.

https://ec.europa.eu/eurostat/statistics-explained/index.php/Agricultural_census_in_Cyprus
An agricultural census is produced every ten years. The most recent, from 2012, contains a number of statistics explaining key crops, land use, and the number of people involved.

https://atlas.media.mit.edu/en/profile/country/cyp
The report from the Observatory of Economic Complexity (OEC) tracks import and export figures, including key trading partners and the main products that are imported and exported.

ENVIRONMENT

Cyprus is known for its olive groves, such as those in the Troodos Mountains, shown here.

CYPRUS IS AN ISLAND, AND SO IT MAY come as a surprise to some that one of the biggest problems facing Cypriot residents and farmers is a lack of water. Repeated periods of drought and ongoing water shortages mean that many parts of the island face ongoing water restrictions. The water supply is safe to drink. However, it is not quality that is the issue but quantity. Lack of rainfall, depleted reservoirs, and contamination from seawater have all made the problem worse.

ENVIRONMENTAL PROBLEMS

Beyond the water shortage, erosion, increased tourism, and rapid growth of coastal cities all threaten Cyprus's coastline. Some stretches of coastline have now been given special protected status in an attempt to prevent further damage.

As cities grow to provide more services for the increasing amount of tourists, the local habitat suffers. Cyprus is home to a large number of species of flora and fauna that cannot be found elsewhere. But some of these now face extinction as their natural habitats shrink.

Steps are being taken to help the environment, but in January 2018, Environment Commissioner Ioanna Panayiotou announced that Cyprus still has a long way to go to meet its own environmental protection guidelines and those established by the European Union. She spoke of the need to focus on sustainable development and the need to develop plans that link economic development with better management of natural resources.

WATER SHORTAGES

From 2004 to 2008, Cyprus underwent its worst water shortage for many years. Although rainfall increased for a time, another period of drought began in 2016 and was ongoing into 2018. These shortages are a result of prolonged dry seasons and lower-than-average rainfall over several years. Since 1972, rainfall has dropped 20 percent, and runoff into reservoirs has dropped dramatically by 40 percent. The situation is expected to continue or worsen, with experts predicting another 10 to 15 percent decline within the next two decades.

The low water levels at the Arminou Reservoir are evidence of Cyprus's ongoing water problems.

Experts believe that Cyprus's water crisis is mainly due to climate change and global warming. Global warming causes the temperature to rise, bringing about droughts and desertification. The lack of water means there is inadequate water for irrigation. It also affects the quality of the soil. Many areas in agriculture, including the widespread growing of Cyprus's symbolic citrus trees, are being threatened because of the water shortage.

Water has always been highly valued in Cyprus, as the people are accustomed to regular periods of drought due to the nation's location and climate. Cypriots are concerned about this severe water shortage because it impacts everyday life as well as the economy, in particular agriculture and tourism. Although agriculture requires huge amounts of water, the growing tourist market provides a greater percentage of the nation's GDP. This often means that water is diverted away from farming areas to coastal resorts.

Cyprus has one of the world's highest concentrations of reservoirs, but as of June 2018, its reservoirs stood only at around 22 percent full. This was a marked improvement from the drought in 2008, when reservoirs held less than half of that. However, officials worried that drought conditions could leave the reservoir supplies depleted by the end of the year unless significant water-saving measures were taken. Cyprus's largest dam, in Kouris, creates a reservoir that can hold about 3 million tons (2.72 million metric tons) of water. It stood at 16.7 percent full. In 2008, it declined to less than 1 percent.

In an attempt to solve its water shortage problems, Cyprus has relied heavily on its desalinization plants, which take water from the sea and purify it, making it fit for human use. However, this solution is not ideal because these desalinization plants are able to supply less than half the water the country needs. The practice of desalinization is also environmentally unfriendly because it consumes large amounts of energy and causes pollution by emitting greenhouse gases into the air.

In the short term, the government of Cyprus has imposed restrictions on water usage on the general public in an attempt to conserve water. In the past, the government has imported water from Greece. Some experts say that unless Cyprus gets used to the low rainfall levels by adapting its methods of farming and managing its water supply more efficiently, it will continue to suffer from a water shortage.

In some areas, the lack of water has caused as many as 50 percent of the trees to die. Without tree cover, the soil becomes parched and of poor quality. This, in turn, may lead to large areas of Cyprus becoming desert if the situation does not improve.

Ongoing drought and lack of rainfall is also a problem in northern Cyprus. One method of tackling the problem there has been to construct a pipeline that imports drinking water from Turkey.

A COASTLINE AT RISK

Cyprus boasts a beautiful coastline with a total coast length of approximately 403 miles (648 km). Unfortunately, the coastline of Cyprus, like the coasts of many other countries in the Mediterranean, is suffering from severe coastal degradation and erosion.

According to the Ministry of Transport, Communications, and Works of Cyprus, some of the major causes of coastal degradation are man-made. These

Increased construction for tourism is placing the Cyprus coastline under greater risk of erosion.

TURKISH WATER PIPELINE

In October 2015, the Turkish Republic of Northern Cyprus Water Supply Project (KKTC Su Temin Projesi) officially opened, providing northern Cyprus with a new supply of plentiful fresh water.

For decades, there had been rumors and suggestions of building a system to deliver water from Turkey to Cyprus. After the partition, the Turkish government started to look more seriously at the possibility, and in 2011 it announced the project as part of its investment in developing northern Cyprus. Two villages in Turkey were displaced so that a dam could be constructed. This dam is the source for the water. The water travels from the dam along the pipeline to another dam near the northern Cyprus town of Girne. More than 50 miles (80 km) of the pipeline travels beneath the Mediterranean Sea, making it the only project of its kind in the world. The entire project cost more than $576 million.

The pipeline is expected to deliver 2.6 billion cubic feet (75 million cubic meters) of water every year for the next thirty to fifty years. Fifty percent of the water is allotted for domestic and industrial uses, while the remaining 50 percent is allotted for agricultural purposes. Land prices in northern Cyprus are increasing because of the improved water supply, and a growing number of families are returning to agriculture.

Some have nicknamed the water "peace water," saying that it will help to improve the economy of northern Cyprus and that it will encourage Greek Cypriots to reach a reunification agreement. Meanwhile, some Greek Cypriots fear that it will give Turkey greater influence over the north. At the same time, some in the north are angry that Turkey seems reluctant to hand control and management of the pipeline to those on the island.

include rapid tourist development, the majority of which takes place in the coastal areas. Extensive beach quarrying; dam construction; sand mining; the building of coastal structures, such as breakwaters; and urban development too close to the shoreline are some of the factors that may have triggered and accelerated coastal erosion.

Continued coastal erosion not only causes ecological and environmental problems. Its effects cause socioeconomic problems as well. For example, a coastal town with critical coastal erosion may start to lose tourists and visitors, thus hurting local jobs and businesses. Loss of extremely valuable land, including recreational and tourist beaches, and damages to urban infrastructure would be devastating for the economy of coastal towns that rely heavily on tourism.

In 1993, the project Coastal Zone Management for Cyprus was launched by the Public Works Department of Cyprus to find ways to stop the severe erosion and improve the quality of the beaches with minimum impact on the environment. At the end of the project, in 1996, master plans were prepared to ensure that the protection and improvement programs continue to be monitored and implemented. Since the master plans have been in existence, several important parallel breakwaters have been built, and illegal groins—fixed structures extended from the sea wall or shore—have been removed in an attempt to stop the erosion. The breakwaters have become rather controversial in recent years, with some experts claiming that they do more harm than good, and that they lower the quality of the water.

In 2000, the Ministry of Transportation, Communications, and Works began to work in partnership with the University of Athens to protect and improve a further three coastal areas—Kato Pyrgos Tillirias, Crysochou Bay, and Zygi-Kiti. Since then, more breakwaters have been constructed. Studies are ongoing to see if they have helped to improve the situation. However, erosion along the coast seems to be continuing at an alarming rate, despite the interventions.

THREATS TO WILDLIFE

Cyprus has a great deal of wildlife and a unique spectrum of flora and fauna. However, an EU report published in 2009 found that in Cyprus many natural

THE AKAMAS PENINSULA

The Akamas Peninsula, situated at the westernmost tip of Cyprus, is a paradise for nature lovers. It covers an area of approximately 42,000 acres (17,000 ha), 17,300 acres (7,000 ha) of which are designated as state forests. The Akamas is well known for its interesting and varied flora and fauna—it boasts six hundred different plant species and more than one hundred different types of birds, mammals, and reptiles, as well as many rare butterflies.

It is also possible to find large areas of near-virgin habitats and vegetation. The coastline is still mostly pristine and is rich in marine life. Green turtles continue to nest on the beaches, and there is the occasional sighting of the rare monk seal. The geology of the area, which consists of many natural habitats, is environmentally important. The Akamas range of hills, with its gorges and caves, is essential for the survival of a wide variety of wildlife, rare vegetation, and plant communities. Species such as the endemic Cyprus white-toothed shrew, hedgehogs, hares, and foxes can be found here, including several species of bats. Unique species of reptilian fauna such as the spiny-footed lizard and the green toad are rare species that can only be found in any significant numbers in Akamas.

However, the influx of huge numbers of tourists has led to the destruction of the very paradise they seek to enjoy. Although tourists make a large contribution to the national economy, their presence also contributes to the spoiling of the landscape. Locals recognize the damage being done, and so a number of environmental organizations and projects have been working in the area with the objective of preserving this stunning wilderness for future generations to learn from and enjoy. In particular, these organizations aim to safeguard the area's biodiversity by overcoming existing and potential threats. Some of these threats include local landowners who want to develop their land for commercial purposes and British forces who use the area for military exercises.

In July 2018, it was announced that local communities on the Akamas Peninsula were working together with the government to create a national park that would protect the area. Locals are quick to emphasize that they welcome tourists but that they must protect the local ecosystem. They say that development and environmental protections need not be mutually exclusive. Instead, they want to find ways that tourism can enhance, rather than destroy, the local landscape.

Protecting the diversity of wildlife in this area of tremendous ecological value is important not just for Cyprus but also for the entire Mediterranean region.

habitats and numerous species of plants and animals were under threat. Both wildlife and the natural environment in Cyprus were not being adequately protected. The report found that only 21 percent of the natural habitats in Cyprus that had been identified as priority habitats were in a healthy condition, and only 18 percent of the species that had been identified as needing conservation were in a satisfactory state. Habitats along the coast of Cyprus, including sand dunes and wetlands, had been found to be in an unfavorable state. In the animal world, certain mammals and snakes could face extinction.

Although Cyprus has adopted an EU Habitat Directive, there continues to be an alarming lack of information and knowledge on the condition of its key species and habitats today. The monitoring schemes that collect data to help ensure these species are properly protected are inadequately maintained.

Some of the primary threats to Cyprus's wildlife are rapid urbanization and overdevelopment, including the building of houses and roads. The growth of tourism has also contributed to the poor state of wildlife in Cyprus today. Other factors include unsatisfactory agricultural and forestry practices.

Although Cyprus is part of various conservation projects, such as Natura 2000 and the Birds and Habitats Directive, much work remains to be done by the government to make sure that policies are being correctly and efficiently implemented. Failure to safeguard the environment can mean a decline in food production and may eventually impact economic prosperity and the welfare of the population. In January 2018, it was proposed that Cyprus's environment commissioner needed to work harder to produce a sustainable environment. This could be done by doing a better job at enforcing laws already in place as part of the Natura 2000 project, a Europe-wide environmental protection network.

Fortunately, several local organizations are engaged in a number of initiatives to help conserve the Cyprus landscape. Friends of the Earth Cyprus has projects to help prevent wild bird trapping and to protect indigenous forests, as well as regular beach cleanups. In 2017, BirdLife Cyprus completed a two-year project to restore valuable wetlands on land used by the British military. Akotiri Marsh is part of the largest wetland system on the island. By restoring it, environmentalists hope to be able to revive the populations of some declining species, such as the long-legged buzzard and the red-footed falcon.

INTERNET LINKS

https://www.climatechangepost.com/cyprus/coastal-erosion
This short piece explains the problems of coastal erosion on Cyprus and suggests some methods of preventing the damage.

https://www.cyprusisland.net/cyprus-peninsulas/akamas -peninsula
This website offers a detailed description of the ecology of the Akamas Peninsula.

https://www.eea.europa.eu/soer-2015/countries/cyprus
In 2015, the European Environment Agency produced this report about the main environmental problems facing Cyprus.

https://blogs.ei.columbia.edu/2010/09/16/cyprus-a-case-study -in-water-challenges
The blog from the Earth Institute at Columbia University explains some of the challenges facing Cyprus with regards to the water supply.

http://blogs.lse.ac.uk/europpblog/2015/10/28/how-turkeys-peace -water-project-could-affect-relations-between-greek-and-turkish -cypriots
This blog examines how the Cyprus "peace water" project could affect Greek-Turkish relations on the island. As water shortages become an ever-increasing problem, can the new pipeline to the north help to improve relations with the south?

CYPRIOTS

The people of Cyprus enjoy new and old traditions. This jazz group performs during the Ayia Napa Festival in 2008.

6

People in Cyprus define themselves both by nationality and heritage, being either Greek Cypriot or Turkish Cypriot.

THE OFFICIAL TOTAL POPULATION OF Cyprus was 1,221,549 in 2017. In the south, Greek Cypriots make up 98.8 percent of the official population, with Turkish Cypriots, Maronites, Armenians, and others making up the remaining 1.2 percent. An official census of northern Cyprus carried out in 2011 claimed a population of 294,000, but this figure has been widely disputed, with some claiming the actual figure to be closer to 700,000. Some say the local government deliberately undercounted in a bid to get financial aid from Turkey. The population in the north is now split fairly evenly between Turkish Cypriots and Turks who resettled there since 1974.

There have been several waves of migration from Cyprus, both following independence in 1960 and after the partition in 1974. There are now sizable Cypriot communities in the United Kingdom, Australia, Canada, and elsewhere. There are an estimated 80,000 Greek Cypriots living in the UK, and approximately 130,000 Turkish Cypriots. The latter figure does not include those born in the UK or of dual heritage; it is believed that would raise the official figure to more than 300,000.

A COMMUNITY DIVIDED

For many centuries, Cypriots lived in ethnically mixed villages, and by appearance it was impossible to tell the two communities apart. Nevertheless, despite four hundred years of largely peaceful cohabitation, cultural and religious differences resulted in little genuine mixing between the two communities. Greek Cypriots remain culturally oriented toward Greece, speak Greek, and practice the Greek Orthodox religion, while most Turkish Cypriots speak Turkish and practice the Islamic religion. Religious differences in particular have made intermarriage difficult and unlikely.

Since the partition of the island, the differences have become more pronounced, while the movement of refugees in both directions has meant that coexistence is virtually unheard of. Although history has created the schism in the Cypriot community, current attitudes further entrench the divide. Ethnic nationalism is rife—Turkish flags fly above many buildings in the north of the island, just as Greece's blue flag with its white cross and stripes adorns every church and public building in the south. The Turks are clearly oriented toward the Turkish mainland, while the Greeks look toward Athens and Europe. Mutual mistrust and linguistic and cultural barriers continue to exist. Few Greek Cypriots now speak Turkish, and the only Turkish Cypriots who speak Greek are a few older people who worked for Greek businesses before 1974.

Although most Turkish and Greek Cypriots moved to their allotted side of the green line (sometimes called the Attila line) following the division of the island in 1974, some small ethnic enclaves exist on both sides of the border. In the north, only 343 Greek Cypriots still live around the village of Dipkarpas (called Rizokarpaso by the Greek Cypriots) on the Karpas Peninsula, the remnants of some twenty thousand Greeks who had lived there before the Turkish invasion. UN peacekeeping forces deliver food and mail from Greek Nicosia; relatives from Greek Cyprus are allowed to visit intermittently. Today, Dipkarpas is also home to a large Kurdish minority. Surprisingly, one biethnic village remains on the island, an example of how Cypriots lived before the partition. Situated where the Attila line buffer zone meets the British base at Dhekelia, the village of Pyla remains a vestige of the past, a perfect microcosm of the island before 1974. Greeks (64 percent) and Turks (36 percent) live in proximity but not always together, socializing in separate coffeehouses and attending separate communal schools. The village has three churches and a mosque.

CYPRIOTS OF GREEK DESCENT

Through the centuries, Greek Cypriots have maintained their Greek identity. The retention of the Greek language and the establishment of the Greek Orthodox religion through the independent Church of Cyprus have become the twin bastions of the Greek Cypriot identity. The Greeks have clung fiercely to their roots because they were subject to constant invasion and conquest by foreign powers in the past. The Ottoman occupation and, more recently, the threat

Men perform a traditional Greek Cypriot dance at a village celebration.

from Turkey have led the Greek Cypriot population to assert their identity even more firmly than they would if they did not feel threatened.

Almost all Greek Cypriots live in the south, and most have been abroad at some time or another. For those who can afford it, overseas education, especially in Greece and Britain, is popular. Most Greek Cypriots speak at least a bit of English. Because of this, Greek Cypriots think of themselves as Europeans, despite their geographical proximity and historical links to the Middle East.

TURKISH BUT NOT TURKISH

Many Turkish Cypriots are descendants of the mainland Turks who remained on the island after the Ottoman conquest in the sixteenth century. During that period, religion rather than ethnicity was the determining civic factor. Thus, many of today's Turkish Cypriots do not trace their lineage to Turkey but to a variety of sources, including the Balkans and Africa. Studies have also suggested that some Turkish Cypriots are, in fact, descendants of Greek Cypriots who converted to Islam during the Ottoman period.

Since 1974, more mainland Turks have settled with their families in Cyprus to work on farms. These settlers are given TRNC citizenship if they remain on the island for more than five years. Turkish immigration has reinforced the Turkish identity of the north and created a stronger relationship with Turkey. However, social tensions have built up over the years. The Turkish Cypriots think that the mainlanders are increasingly controlling the economy and dictating the north's relations with the international community. They also believe that the steady influx of mainland Turks is slowly diluting the Turkish Cypriot identity, making them more Anatolian in character. In 2005, the TRNC tightened its control over Turkish immigration following an increase in crime and unemployment. This caused the first major disagreement between the TRNC and Turkey. Since then, the relationship between the two groups has been filled with ups and downs. On the one hand, the Turkish Cypriots were able to shrug off the financial crisis that affected Greece and much of Europe since they were not tied to the European markets. They have also benefited greatly from the newly built water pipeline. On the other hand, mainland

Turkey maintains control of the pipeline, and Turkish Cypriots have expressed some dissatisfaction that they are not allowed more autonomy over their own part of the island.

CLOTHING

Traditional dress is an important aspect of Cyprus's traditional culture, although today it is only worn on festive occasions. Cotton and silk, and a blend of the two called *itare* (IH-tahr-eh), are the main materials used. Silkworms are bred on the island, and most materials are woven in the home. Traditionally, the best festival dress is associated with marriage practices, especially dowry ceremonies. Items worn by the bridegroom, such as a silk handkerchief, are offered as a gift to his fiancée.

Compared to the dress of their mainland Greek compatriots, the clothes of Greek Cypriots are simpler and more uniform. For women, two styles are most popular. The *karpasitiko* (karp-ahs-IHT-ih-koh) includes a long-sleeved white

A young girl wears a traditional Turkish Cypriot costume.

dress with a high, round neck. Full white trousers, either plain or embroidered, are worn underneath the dress. A long, tight-fitting coat with decorated sleeves is worn over the top. The front of the coat is low-cut, to reveal the dress. On her head, a woman wears an embroidered white or colored handkerchief, either draped or folded. Another popular choice is a black velvet, long-sleeved jacket worn over a long cotton shirt with a long, checked or striped skirt. A red fez or white handkerchief is worn on the head. Low-heeled black shoes are worn with both types of clothing. Men's traditional dress includes a long-sleeved white shirt and full, baggy black trousers tucked into black boots. A black sash is tied around the waist, and an embroidered black vest is worn over the shirt. A small black cap is worn on the back of the head.

For Turkish Cypriots, traditional dress derived from mainland Turkey is worn on festive occasions. Men will wear a red fez, and parts of the body are stained with red henna. Religion and custom decree that no hair should be seen, so both men and women wear a headdress. Not too long ago, women covered their faces with veils or draped scarves too.

The basic dress has remained the same for many centuries—baggy trousers, called *shalvar* (shahl-VAHR), are worn by the women, along with a vest or a high-necked, calf-length jacket. Men also wear the *shalvar*, most often colored black or blue. Short, embroidered vests, called *cepken* (chep-KEHN), are worn over high-necked white shirts. Leather sandals with turned-up toes are worn by both men and women.

MAKING A HOME IN CYPRUS

Inevitably, because of the island's checkered and turbulent history, many other people have settled in Cyprus over the centuries. Although most have assimilated into the Greek or Turkish communities, a few groups, such as the Maronites and Armenians, retain a distinct identity. There is also a very small group of Syrian refugees who have resettled in Cyprus. One hundred forty-three people were relocated there from Greece and Italy in 2017, and another ten families were welcomed in 2018. Cyprus's Roma community remains largely unstudied, but the population is estimated to number about three hundred.

THE ARMENIAN COMMUNITY

There is currently a population of roughly 3,500 Armenians living on Cyprus. Most of them live in or near Nicosia, but there are also small communities in several other cities. As an officially recognized minority, they maintain their own language and churches, and have their own schools. Trade ties between Armenia and Cyprus date back as far as the sixth century CE. When Armenia was brought under the influence of the Byzantine Empire, as many as ten thousand Armenians were forcibly settled in Cyprus by the Byzantine emperors to work the land. As fellow Christians, the Armenians had few problems assimilating into Greek Cypriot culture.

During and after World War I, more than 1.5 million Armenians were murdered and hundreds of thousands more were driven from their homeland by the Ottoman Empire. Some made their way to Cyprus, which was one of the first nations to recognize the Armenian genocide. A memorial to those who lost their lives stands in Larnaca.

Today, they remain a small but active and important voice in Cypriot society. Because they are designated a religious group, like Maronites, they are allowed one representative in government. However, the representative has no voting power. A campaign is under way to be recognized as a community rather than a religious group. Armenian Cypriots argue this would give them a greater voice in politics.

Notable Armenian Cypriots include Benon Sevan (former assistant secretary-general of the United Nations), poet Nora Nadjarian, and pop singer Hovig Demirjian.

MARONITES

Maronites are an Arab people from Lebanon who practice a form of Catholicism. They first came to Cyprus with the Lusignan Crusaders in the twelfth century, serving as archers against the Arabs. Saint Maron, a Syrian hermit of the late fourth century, and later Saint John Maron, the patriarch of Antioch from 685 to 707, are the founders of the Maronite religion.

Many expatriates move to Cyprus for the good climate, relaxed way of life, and excellent standard of living.

Cyprus has a notable expatriate population, mostly people from Northern Europe who have chosen to retire or set up a business there. Holiday homes and villas have been built in many parts of southern Cyprus to cater to the influx of people seeking to enjoy the island's dry, warm climate and relaxed atmosphere. The Cypriot government's favorable tax concessions and improvements in the infrastructure have helped this development. Cyprus's membership in the European Union in May 2004 also allowed nationals of any EU state the right to reside in Cyprus for up to three months. Many British nationals have settled there, mainly in the south around Limassol. Current estimates vary widely, but more reliable figures say that there are about twenty-four thousand British people now residing in the republic. Some own bars and restaurants around the popular tourist areas of Limassol, Ayia Napa, and Paphos, while some operate offshore businesses or are connected with the British military. Many of these people have come to Cyprus to retire in a country that retains strong economic and cultural links with Britain. Britain maintains military bases in Cyprus, where English is widely spoken. Many Germans and Scandinavians have also chosen to make Cyprus their home. There are also many Lebanese, Arab, Iranian, Russian, and Serbian entrepreneurs living in Limassol and Nicosia, usually running offshore banking and other services linked to interests in the Middle East and Eastern Europe.

The British military bases near Limassol and Larnaca give the two towns a very British feel at times, especially during the tourist season. The bases of Akrotiri and Dhekelia are miniature Britains, with pubs, housing developments, golf courses, and military hospitals to serve the military community. Most British soldiers are well behaved and are appreciated for the money that they spend in the bars, restaurants, and clubs on the island, but fights between soldiers and locals, and soldiers and tourists, occasionally occur. More serious incidents are very rare, but when they do occur, they can stir up tensions between the military and the local people.

In the north, foreign presence is far less noticeable. In the early and mid-twentieth century, the town of Kyrenia was a popular retirement place for former colonial officials. Before the Turkish invasion, some two thousand expatriates, mainly British, lived in Kyrenia. By 1976, most had fled, and only two hundred remained. With the establishment of peace and the growth of tourism, this number has increased in the last few decades. Today, Kyrenia remains a popular choice for British expatriates. According to a 2016 newspaper article, an estimated five thousand to fifteen thousand British people now live in northern Cyprus.

Korucam (Kormacit in Turkish), north of Morphou, is the Cypriot Maronite capital, though only a few hundred Maronites still live in the village. They worship at a church in the village, Ayios Georgios, without interference from the Turkish authorities. Since the partition, most Maronites have moved to the south to seek a better life, and the community in Korucam is steadily declining. Maronites speak their native tongue, which is a dialect of Arabic mixed with many Greek and Turkish words.

This is the Maronite cathedral in Nicosia. Maronites form just a small percentage of the population on Cyprus.

INTERNET LINKS

http://adoulotishakalli.com/costumes
The Refugee Folkloric Group has a series of detailed illustrated descriptions of traditional costumes of Cyprus.

https://cyprus-mail.com/2017/06/26/armenians-like-officially-designated-community
A newspaper article describes how Armenians would like to be officially designated as a community in Cyprus so that they may have a voting voice in government.

http://www.maronite-institute.org/MARI/JMS/july99/The_Maronites_of_Cyprus.htm
This article describes the Maronite community of Cyprus, including their history and their religion.

LIFESTYLE

Much of Cyprus remains very rural and agricultural.

CYPRIOT RURAL LIFE WAS unchanged for many centuries, even as the world outside changed dramatically. The men in the family would raise crops or livestock, while the women raised a family and managed the home. However, in the latter part of the twentieth century, increased economic prosperity and outside influences saw Cyprus in greater contact with the rest of Europe. This led to some changes within society. Women's roles have changed somewhat, although they are now expected to juggle household responsibilities and work. People tend to stay in school longer, and many travel overseas or move to the cities. As a result, the rural way of life is rapidly declining in some areas.

The average life expectancy in Cyprus is 78.8 years (81.8 years for women and 76 years for men). The crime rate is extremely low on both sides of the divide. Major offenses, such as assault or murder, occur rarely,

7

As in many Mediterranean countries, the people of Cyprus take a siesta during the middle of the day and work into the cooler hours of the evening.

and theft has traditionally been virtually unheard of. Although petty theft and residential burglaries have increased in recent years, rates still remain much lower than elsewhere in Europe. A small rise in organized crime has seen outbreaks of violence between opposing groups. In the north, sex trafficking and forced labor of migrants is becoming a problem needing to be addressed and eliminated.

RURAL LIFE

Before the Turkish invasion in 1974, there were more than six hundred villages in Cyprus. The village was the core of Cypriot life for both Greeks and Turks. In bicommunal villages, Muslim minarets and church bell towers formed the same skyline. Today, there are fewer and fewer inhabited villages where the traditional rural lifestyle remains. Despite this decline, village life is still important to many older Cypriots and is inextricably linked to notions of Cypriot identity.

MOVE TO THE CITIES

Since the 1960s, there has been a very pronounced drift from village to town all over Cyprus, a trend accelerated by the ethnic conflicts and partition of the island. Cypriots are traditionally rural people. Before 1931, only 22 percent of Cypriots lived in a town, and until 1974, more than half the population lived in villages. Today, approximately 67 percent of people living in both the north and the south live in urban areas. Urbanization is increasing at a rate of nearly 1 percent per year. The average age of the inhabitants in some of the more remote villages in the Troodos Mountains is increasing, suggesting that many villages may become deserted in the future. In the 1960s, it was common for village residents to commute to the towns to work, since most villages were within an hour's travel to one of the six towns. However, a series of factors has led to a rapid expansion of the towns. They include the need for new housing created by the refugees who settled in Cyprus following the Turkish invasion, the increased modernization of life, especially in the south, the massive building boom, and the development of the coast-based tourist industry.

Expectations for Cypriots have risen sharply. Apart from the influence of tourist development, the harsh village life has led many young Cypriots to look for better lives in the towns. Greater educational opportunities and a higher standard of living encouraged younger Cypriots to seek more than the simple rural life of earlier generations. The Paphos district, for example, had been a rural backwater offering few opportunities. During the 1960s and 1970s, many Cypriots from the district migrated to other regions, since Paphos had limited work on the plantations along the coast. The Turks left after the 1974 invasion, further reducing the population by one-quarter, leaving many former Turkish villages deserted. Most of the young people work as hotel receptionists, bar staff, and cooks, suggesting that although the district is now prospering, vital, traditional links with the rural way of life are being lost.

The Cypriot government has introduced many plans to improve agricultural life and rural infrastructure, such as irrigation projects and building local schools, in an attempt to promote the village lifestyle and protect the rural heritage. In 2007, the Cyprus Tourism Organization launched a program called "Rural Tourism" to promote the attractions and culture of the countryside. Another program, overseen in the country by the Cyprus Sustainable Tourism Initiative and started as a partnership encompassing institutions and networks in six European nations in 2010, was Women Entrepreneurs in Rural Tourism

Nicosia is the largest city on the island and is important to both northern and southern Cyprus.

The coffeehouse—kahve (kah-VEH) in Turkish, or kapheneia (gahf-EHN-ee-ah) in Greek—is a permanent and defining aspect of the life of the island, especially in the villages. Coffeehouses are mostly male-dominated establishments. Sitting in coffeehouses and discussing the issues of the world—whether those are money, soccer, weather, or politics—is the favorite pastime of most Cypriot men. Commonly located in the village square, the coffeehouse provides a public meeting place for the men of the community to discuss local issues, relax, and exchange gossip. Men will often spend many hours playing backgammon or card games. Increasingly, coffee  *shops are also equipped with television, though the television is generally turned on only for soccer games or movies. Before the partition, most villages had two coffeehouses, one for the Turkish community and one for the Greek, but today this is no longer necessary.*

Hospitality is the hallmark of the coffeehouse, and strangers who hesitate at the door will generally be invited in. The coffeehouses are usually open all day, and often the men will gather there early in the morning before starting work for a quick cup of coffee. At the end of the day, they will also settle down at the coffeehouse for another cup. Coffeehouses sell mainly coffee and cold drinks, including beer and spirits. The coffee is normally very strong and drunk in small quantities, accompanied by a glass of water to wash it down. In the evening, the men might switch to brandy. In small, isolated villages, the coffeehouse even serves as a local store and post office.

Coffeehouses are often seen as men's spaces, and even today women are not allowed in some.

(WERT). The program ran from 2010 until 2012 and provided assistance to women in rural communities who wished to start their own businesses in areas that would both help to attract tourists and benefit the local community—for example, arts and crafts or food production. Programs such as WERT enrich and rejuvenate communities from within, rather than from outside.

The typical Cypriot village consists of a series of narrow roads and tracks linking outlying farms to the village. The village itself is centered around the village square. In the square, there will probably be a church or mosque, depending on whether the village is Greek or Turkish; a coffeehouse; and a number of stores. Men tend to begin work at dawn, often finishing their farm chores by midday. Irrigating the crops is an essential daily activity on this sun-parched island, and it is the difference between success and failure for the farmer. Stocks of water and underground reservoirs are constantly monitored. The coffee shop is the fulcrum of the village for the men, where news and gossip are exchanged. Traditionally, women are excluded from this activity and are usually found either looking after the family or working in the fields. Even old women will help bring in the harvest and tend the livestock. Nevertheless, life is not just about work for Cypriot women. They often sit in shady backstreets to embroider, knit, and gossip. On the weekends, villages burst into activity. The extended family gathers to eat and exchange news, and the taverns and coffee shops are at their liveliest. During festival times, processions, feasting, music, and dancing transform the village, bringing it to life.

Hospitality is one of the cornerstones of the Cypriot way of life, and Cypriots are usually generous and gracious hosts. Turkish Cypriots are far less exposed to foreigners than their Greek counterparts, and they consequently treat guests, or in Turkish, *misafir* (mihs-ah-FEER), with lavish cordiality and generosity. Typically, Turkish Cypriots will ply their guests with food and drink, especially coffee.

A village in the Troodos Mountains. Many villages are shrinking as younger people move to the cities.

DWELLINGS

The traditional rural dwellings of Cyprus have maintained the same character for many centuries. Most of them are functional because farmers believe that dwellings should only be big enough to accommodate their inhabitants, while the surrounding land should stretch as far as the eye can see. The houses are built around a courtyard, with a beehive-shaped clay oven in the center.

In the towns of the south, modern dwellings are two-story, airy buildings built in a style found throughout the Mediterranean. The centers of Limassol and Larnaca are dominated by high-rise buildings, an increasingly familiar sight throughout Cyprus. Many wealthy Cypriots and expatriates build villas for themselves on the edge of the towns. The urban areas have rapidly expanded, swallowing many smaller villages in the process.

FAMILY LIFE

The family has always been an important part of Cypriot society, for both the Greek community and the Turkish Cypriot community. When Cypriots speak of their families, they do not only mean their immediate relations; the family circle extends to second cousins and further. Families are a great source of support and pride, and kinship links are kept religiously. Family members are obliged to help one another at any time and in any way possible, including lending money, helping with employment or establishing business contacts, building homes, or finding suitable marriage partners.

Cypriot parents are willing to sacrifice a great deal for their children, and no expense is spared in ensuring that they attain a high level of education. Traditionally, marriages were arranged in Cyprus, but this custom is now rarely practiced. It is more common now for the young to choose their own partners. After marriage, women are expected to look after the house and rear children, and leisure activities are limited to watching television and visiting relatives. Although these restrictions are not as widespread in modern Cyprus as they were in the past, much of this traditional morality lingers, and women have to be careful of their behavior.

Men, on the other hand, are the breadwinners and heads of the household, and they are allowed, and expected, to pursue their own entertainment and pleasure. When compared to many other countries in Europe, Cyprus is still very much a male-dominated society, and women are characterized in conservative terms. However, many women today have paid jobs, and they are making inroads into even traditional male occupations, such as politics and the law. Greater economic independence has helped free them somewhat from the restrictions of traditional, sex-designated roles. Nevertheless, although divorce statistics are rising, marriage is still the life choice for the vast majority of young Cypriots.

Since 1998, in line with EU laws, homosexuality has been made legal in the Republic of Cyprus, and gay life does exist, but only in the tourist areas.

Since Cyprus has traditionally been a rural society, women's roles have been centered upon the family and the home. Until relatively recently, women entered into marriage partnerships that had been arranged by their fathers. They rarely worked outside the home, and the husband was head of the household.

During the British occupation, some educational and workplace opportunities opened up, but only in the last few decades have women begun to make marked progress. Now the employment rate for women is 69 percent. As women stay longer in education, they are also delaying marriage and starting a family. The average age of a woman having her first child is now twenty-eight years of age.

With more women in the workplace, attention has turned to reducing the gender pay gap. As of 2013, the pay gap between men and women had reduced to 15.8 percent. However, this was more a result of the economic crisis seeing a loss of jobs in male sectors such as construction rather than improvements for women. Equal pay legislation was introduced in 2009.

More women are also entering politics. Although Cyprus remains far behind many other EU member nations, in 2016 the nation boasted its largest ever number of women in elected positions, with 20 percent of parliamentary seats being held by women. Despite this progress, women are still expected to manage the household and family, leading to additional work at the end of the traditional workday.

For the most part, Cyprus remains a socially conservative country where homosexuality is seen as immoral. However, attitudes are changing and becoming more tolerant. In December 2015, civil unions became legal, and in 2017, the government announced that it was drafting a transgender rights bill. Homosexuality was made legal in northern Cyprus in 2014, largely due to pressure from Turkey and other surrounding European nations. Proposals to accept civil unions have not yet been passed.

SCHOOL

This child plays while at school in Cyprus.

The average educational career, from primary to tertiary education, is fourteen years for males and fifteen years for females. Cyprus spends 6.1 percent of its GDP on education, ranking it nineteenth in the world for expenditure. The literacy rate is 99.5 percent among males and 98.7 percent among females.

In the south, one year of pre-primary education is compulsory. All children must begin pre-primary education by the time they are aged four years and eight months. Many begin as early as three years of age. Elementary education is mandatory and free for all children from age five to twelve. Free secondary education lasts for another six years. This includes three years at a gymnasium or a preparatory college and three years in high school. Only three years of this are compulsory, as children may leave school at the age of fifteen. There are state universities as well as many private universities available in the country. However, an education overseas is still the choice of many Cypriots, with up to ten thousand going abroad each year, especially to Britain and Greece.

In the Turkish north, education is free and compulsory for all children from age seven to fifteen. Further education is provided for sixteen- to eighteen-year-olds at high schools. Higher education is state-provided. Universities include the Eastern Mediterranean University near Famagusta and the Cyprus International University.

WORK LIFE

The Greek Cypriot school year runs from September through May, with school from Monday to Friday, starting at 7:30 a.m. and ending at 1:35 p.m. All students wear a uniform of gray pants or skirt with a white, gray, or black T-shirt.

Working hours throughout the island revolve around the Mediterranean siesta. Typically, shops are open from 8:00 a.m. to 1:00 p.m. and 2:30 p.m. to 5:30 p.m. in the winter, and from 7:30 a.m. to 1:00 p.m. and 4:00 p.m. to 7:00 p.m. in the summer. The Cypriot government operates a comprehensive social insurance program that covers all working adults and their dependents. Benefits from the program cover unemployment, sickness, maternity leave, injury at work, and old-age pension. All contributions to the program are income-related. Workers are protected against unjust dismissal. Unemployment rates in the

Greek portion of Cyprus rose because of the financial collapse. Current rates are approximately 11.8 percent, a notable increase from 3.9 percent one decade earlier.

In the north, although official statistics continue to suggest a relatively low rate of unemployment, there is considerable underemployment, particularly in farming. Most people work but do not have quite enough to be prosperous. As a result of regular high inflation, a minimum wage is fixed by law for all occupations and determined by a commission including the government and employers. A cost-of-living allowance is also paid to offset the effects of high inflation. However, although government bodies pay the allowance regularly, private companies do not. This has led to public sector employees becoming wealthier than their private sector counterparts. With the opening of the borders in 2003, it is estimated that thousands of Turkish workers travel to work in the south each day through the British base in Dhekelia. Although some work on the base, many travel farther to work on building sites in the south. Others work in temporary or seasonal jobs as waiters or cleaners. A large number of Turkish Cypriots also use the airport in Larnaca to fly to other European cities to seek work.

Businesses close and the streets empty during the traditional afternoon siesta.

INTERNET LINKS

http://www.country-data.com/cgi-bin/query/r-3511.html
This description of traditional family life focuses on Turkish Cypriots.

http://countrystudies.us/cyprus/24.htm
Here one has a look at family and marriage in Cyprus, in particular changes that took place in society after World War II and toward the end of the twentieth century.

http://www.highereducation.ac.cy/en/educational-system.html
This website offers an explanation of the education system in Cyprus, from preschool to post-secondary education, produced by the Ministry of Education and Culture.

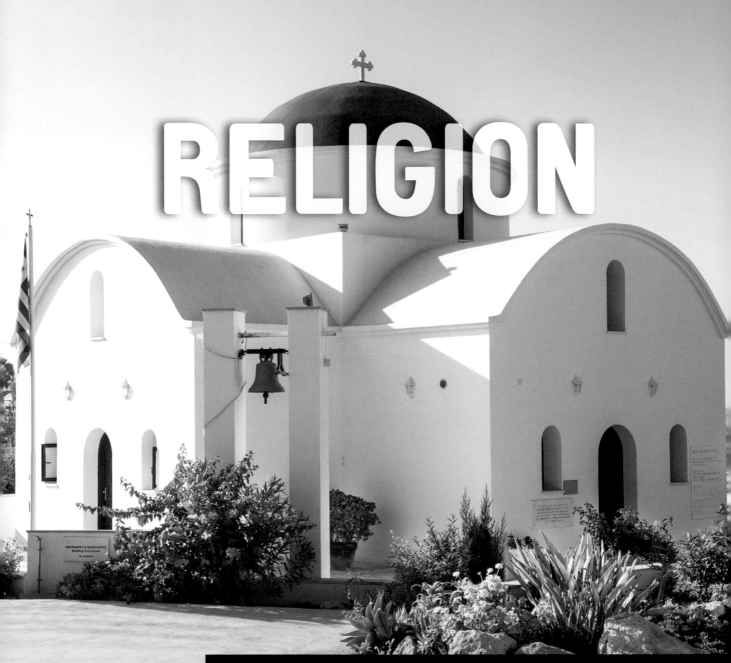

RELIGION

Throughout the southern part of the country, many people attend Orthodox Christian churches, such as this one.

AS MIGHT BE EXPECTED GIVEN THE long and varied history of Cyprus, there are a number of different religions to be found scattered throughout the island. In the larger cities, you can see a Greek Orthodox church on one corner, a mosque farther down the street, and perhaps a small Armenian church just a few blocks away.

In the southern republic, 89 percent of the population is Greek Orthodox, 3 percent is Roman Catholic, 2 percent is Protestant, and 2 percent is Muslim. The remaining population is a combination of Buddhist, Armenian Christian, Maronite, Hindu, and other faiths. In the north, the majority of the population is Muslim, with a small percentage of Maronites, Greek Orthodox, and Armenian Christians.

Since the island was partitioned in 1974, it has become much more segregated by religion. Prior to partition, the south had a greater number of Muslims and the north had more churches. Now, many churches in the north have either been demolished or converted to mosques. In the south, there are still mosques in the larger cities. Those in more rural areas have been closed and lie unused.

ORTHODOX CHRISTIANITY

The huge number of Orthodox churches throughout the island and the beauty of the frescoes and icons inside them bear testimony to the island's strong Orthodox Christian traditions. The majority of Cyprus's Greeks are

It is mentioned in Acts 13 of the Bible that Cyprus was Saint Paul's first missionary destination. Born in Tarsus, under the name Saul, Saint Paul, together with the apostle Barnabas, set sail to Cyprus from Seleucia. It was after his departure from Cyprus that he changed his name to Paul. In Cyprus, Paul and Barnabas first went to Salamis, then traveled throughout the entire island preaching and proclaiming the word of God in synagogues. When they reached Paphos, they met the magician Elymas, also known as Bar-Jesus, who was a Jewish false prophet. The magician opposed them when they attempted to preach the word of God to the Roman proconsul, Sergius Paulus. However, Paul rebuked Elymas and blinded him temporarily, thus  *allowing them to successfully convert Sergius Paulus to Christianity. However, according to the Bible, before Paul was able to make Sergius Paulus believe in the teachings of Christianity, the local pagans lashed him to a marble pillar and "scourged him thirty-nine times." This pillar is now known as Saint Paul's Pillar, and it is now a famous tourist attraction in Paphos.*

One of the island's most famous monasteries is named after Saint Barnabas, companion of Saint Paul and one of those responsible for bringing Christianity to Cyprus. Barnabas was born in Salamis and is revered as the founder of the Cypriot church. The details about Barnabas's later life are uncertain, but he is traditionally thought to have been martyred by stoning in around 61 CE.

The discovery of Barnabas's bones buried beneath a carob tree on the Mesaoria Plain in the late fifth century provides the Church of Cyprus a foundation on which to claim its ecclesiastical independence. After the apostle's remains were unearthed, the archbishop of Cyprus went to Constantinople to ask for the Cypriot church to be granted autonomous status. The Byzantine emperor Zeno agreed, persuaded by the gift of the original copy of the Gospel of Saint Matthew, supposedly handwritten by Barnabas and found clasped in the dead saint's arms. The tomb of Barnabas is at the Monastery of Apostolos Varnavas (Barnabas), situated north of Famagusta. Cypriots of all faiths still revere the location.

Orthodox Christians, a part of the Eastern Orthodox faith that is dominant in Greece, Russia, and much of Eastern Europe. However, Cypriots have their own independent church, the Orthodox Church of Cyprus. Although similar in practice to the Greek Orthodox Church, the Church of Cyprus is not under the authority of an external patriarch. In 488 CE, the Byzantine emperor Zeno granted this independent status to Archbishop Anthemius. Since the eighteenth century, the Cypriot clergy has played a prominent social and political role on the island, mainly as a result of the Ottoman style of rule that gave both secular and religious authority to the clergy. Consequently, the archbishop of Cyprus was also given the title of "ethnarch," or national leader of the Greek community. The archbishop is elected by representatives of the towns and villages of Cyprus.

Orthodox worship is highly visual, and ritual plays an important role. Orthodox churches are richly decorated with religious art, including icons, frescoes, murals, and ecclesiastical vessels. The intention is to provide strong visual encouragement for the worshippers, stimulating faith and piety. Icons are positioned around the inside of most churches, and walls are covered with frescoes depicting religious events and symbolizing religious ideas. An iconostasis—a highly decorated partition that divides the sanctuary from the rest of the church—is also a part of Orthodox worship. The congregation looks into the sanctuary through doorways in the iconostasis. On each side of the doorways are icons representing Jesus Christ, the Virgin Mary, the Four Evangelists, and the Last Supper. Symbolically, the iconostasis represents a religious presence during services, a filter through which the faithful may worship. Orthodox believers always pray standing, light candles as offerings, and often kiss the icons as a sign of respect and supplication. The combined experience is intended to convey the mysterious essence of the faith. The priest will wear garments that have symbolic meaning.

THE ISLAMIC FAITH

Cyprus's Turkish minority is almost exclusively made up of Sunni Muslims. Authority for the Muslim religion in Cyprus is the mufti, an expert in Islamic law, and the Quran, the Muslim holy book. Generally, the Muslims in Cyprus are

Easter is by far the biggest festival in the Republic of Cyprus, with huge carnivals held to celebrate the end of the Lenten fast.

Monasticism is a long-established and essential feature of the Orthodox tradition, growing out the Roman emperor Constantine's unification of state and church. Cypriots are proud of their monastic traditions and institutions, especially the magnificent hilltop monasteries of Kykkos, Machairas, and Stavrovouni. The monasteries have borne the ideals of Orthodox Christendom through time despite numerous foreign invasions and occupations. Cyprus  *contributes more monks to the monastic enclave of Mount Athos, the most important center of Orthodoxy in northern Greece, than any other Orthodox country.*

Although their numbers are falling, people still join monasteries. The Stavrovouni monastery, near Larnaca, is considered the strictest one on Cyprus. The monks living here maintain the traditional monastic lifestyle. Most have to be highly committed to a life that makes great demands on them. Their day is divided equally between prayer and study, physical labor, and rest. During the rest periods, the monks eat two frugal meals without meat, and they carry out nightly prayers that constantly interrupt their sleep. The main liturgies (prayers) of the day are practiced in the courtyard. They include predawn "matins," the main liturgy after sunrise, "vespers" before the evening meal, and "compline" later in the evening. Winters in the monastery are very severe, making the monks' farming activities difficult. The monks still paint icons, which are of a very high standard, while many monasteries produce their own wine and make their own jam and honey. The Stavrovouni monastery is open to only male visitors. No women may enter it.

Other monasteries, such as Ayios Neophytos near Paphos, are popular places of pilgrimage where all are welcome. Ayios Neophytos was established by Neophytos, a local saint, in the twelfth century. Neophytos, who had come to the hills of Paphos to seek solitude, cut a hermitage into the rocks with his own hands. Soon a sizeable community sprang up around the famous monk, who was revered for his holiness and wisdom. He was a scholar of considerable note, and his handbook on monastic life, Ritual Ordinance, *survives to this day. Today, pilgrims come to see the bones of the monk in the cave hermitage and to view the beautiful religious frescoes painted by followers of Neophytos.*

not as devout as their mainland counterparts. Islam has never been politically or socially dominant on the island. This can partly be explained by the mixed background of the island's Muslim community, who had intermarried with both Lusignan and Venetian Christians. In the Ottoman period, a sect called Linovamvaki practiced Islam outwardly but maintained Christian beliefs in private.

A number of high-profile Islamic sects have prospered in northern Cyprus. The best known was the Naqshbandi-Haqqani order of Sufism, led by the charismatic Mehmet Nazim Adil until his death in 2014. His home and the headquarters of his organization—the Turkish Cypriot Islamic Society—are in Lefke, near Morphou Bay. There are also groups abroad, including London. The society campaigns for greater piety in the lax religious atmosphere of the north and stresses the authority of the spiritual leader.

Other sects included the thirteenth-century Mevlevi Order, which stressed music and dance as a way of expressing love for God. It lasted until 1954. The Bahai sect from Iran has also had substantial support, particularly in northern Cyprus. Given these unconventional influences, it is not surprising that Turkish Cypriots are not particularly orthodox Muslims. The more obvious expressions of Islamic devotion, such as wearing religious dress and growing long beards, are not popular with Turkish Cypriots. Islamic law, or sharia, is not practiced in northern Cyprus or in Turkey.

Islamic principles differ slightly from those of Christians. Although Muslims believe that the Bible is a sacred book and recognize the teachings of the biblical prophets, they do not believe Jesus is divine; instead, they believe he is a prophet. Muslims consider Muhammad the greatest and final prophet, the carrier of God's message to humankind. However, they do not worship Muhammad, only God, and God's revelations to Muhammad are contained in the Quran. Before beginning prayer, Muslims first wash their hands, arms, feet, ankles, head, and neck in running water. If water is not available, the ritual motions will suffice. They must then cover their head, face Mecca, and perform a precise series of genuflections.

Muslims in Cyprus have traditionally been more liberal than most other Muslim populations. Many Turkish Cypriots drink alcohol, and women are not expected to wear head scarves. In addition, they may only attend mosque services on special occasions such as weddings and funerals. A lot of Cypriot Muslims describe themselves as Cypriots first, Muslims second.

In recent years, Turkish influence has been growing in northern Cyprus, and part of that growing influence has been an increasing emphasis on religion. In 2014, the Hala Sultan Tekke mosque was built in Famagusta. It is the largest of its type in the eastern Mediterranean region. Many locals worry that it is part of an effort to force them to become stricter in their faith. Religious schools have also been introduced.

As a result, Turkish Cypriots have concerns about the future of their culture. Many worry that enforcing stricter Muslim laws will make reunification with the south less likely.

OTHER CHRISTIAN FAITHS

Maronite Christians come from Lebanon, where the Maronite Church is one of the largest eastern branches of the Roman Catholic Church. There are about five thousand Maronite worshippers in Cyprus, according to census data from 2011. Most of them live in the south of Cyprus and have in part assimilated into the Greek Cypriot community. The church traces its origins to Saint Maron, a fourth-century Syrian hermit. The immediate spiritual leader of the Maronite Church, after the pope, is the patriarch of Antioch, who lives in Bkirki, near Beirut. The patriarch of Antioch remains head of the Catholic churches in the Middle East. Despite attempts by the pope to standardize Maronite rites into Latin in accordance with the rest of the Catholic world, the church retains the ancient West Syrian liturgy, although the vernacular language of the Maronites is Arabic. For some years, the Maronites of Cyprus have celebrated Easter at the same time as the island's Orthodox community (typically later than for Roman Catholics), in part because it is convenient.

There are also a few thousand practicing Roman Catholics in Cyprus. Catholicism has a long history on the island. Under Lusignan rule, Catholicism was the religion of the local aristocracy. Many of the island's great religious buildings date from this time. They include the Saint Sophia Cathedral in Nicosia, the Saint Nicholas Cathedral in Famagusta, and the Bellapais Abbey near Kyrenia. All of these buildings have since been converted to mosques or Orthodox institutions.

A Maronite Catholic mass is held to celebrate a special feast day.

There are approximately 3,300 Armenians in Cyprus who practice the Armenian Apostolic faith. The Armenian Apostolic Church was founded in the late third century CE by Gregory the Illuminator, its patron saint and official head. In converting the Armenian king, Gregory in effect created the world's first truly Christian state. The Armenian Church separated from the other Eastern churches in the sixth century and is completely autonomous. It is headed by the Catholicos of Echmiadzin, near Yerevan, in Armenia. Catholicos is the title given to the head of the Armenian Church, and Echmiadzin was the former capital of the Kingdom of Armenia between the second and fourth centuries.

Estimates for the number of Anglicans in Cyprus range from five hundred to a few thousand. They are sustained by the island's small British population.

INTERNET LINKS

http://www.cnewa.org/default.aspx?ID=22&pagetypeID=9&sitecode=hq&pageno=1
This website provides information about the Church of Cyprus's history.

https://www.islammuslimcyprus.com/history-of-islam-in-cyprus.html
This history of Islam in Cyprus includes when Islam was first introduced and how the population grew through history.

LANGUAGE

Depending where they live on the island, these boys may speak Cypriot Greek, Turkish, English … or even all three.

THE TWO PRIMARY LANGUAGES OF Cyprus are Greek (in the south) and Turkish (in the north). However, they are both specific dialects that sound quite different than the language spoken in their country of origin. While a Greek-speaking Cypriot will be able to understand standard Greek, a Greek may find many words on Cyprus unrecognizable. Experts estimate that 15 percent of the words in Cypriot Greek and Turkish are found only on the island. Another odd but interesting fact is that Cypriot Greek and Turkish may both sound like the same language to an outsider. In reality, they are very different, but intonation and accents give them a similar sound.

Because of the past British occupation, English is still widely spoken and understood in the south. Since the British military still has a presence on the island and a large number of British expatriates and tourists visit, the language has retained a strong presence. The ability to speak it still carries a certain amount of prestige among Cyprus natives.

9

Greek and Turkish are the official languages of Cyprus, although English and Russian are also widely spoken.

The sign for this coffeeshop is in both Greek and English.

A few other languages can be found among Cyprus's smaller ethnic groups. These include Armenian, Cypriot Arabic (spoken by the Maronite community and very closely linked to biblical Aramaic), and Kurbetcha (the language of the Roma community).

THE GREEK LANGUAGE

Greek is an Indo-European language that can be traced back to the fourteenth century BCE, making it one of the oldest languages in the world. Many of the writing systems used today are based on ancient Greek. In ancient times, Greek was widely spoken throughout the eastern Mediterranean.

Although the majority of the Greek Cypriot population spoke Greek, a local dialect has developed over many centuries. To some mainlanders, the dialect seems to be a completely different language. Certain sounds in standard Greek are almost completely absent from Cypriot Greek, while in some regional dialects, such as in Paphos, the spoken language has been heavily influenced by Turkish words.

Greek is not an easy language to learn. The positioning of stress is an important part of speaking Greek, and emphasizing the correct syllable is essential for clear communication. An incorrect stress will render words unintelligible, or possibly change their meaning altogether. For example, the word *yéros* (YEH-ros), with a stress on the "e," means "old man," while the same sounds with a stress on the "o," as in *yerós* (yeh-ROS), means "sturdy." Greek has a number of longer vowel sounds, where two vowels appear side by side. The two vowels are usually read together as a single sound. However, if an accent is placed above the first vowel, the two sounds are pronounced separately, and the first vowel sound is given emphasis. Despite these difficulties, Greek is a very beautiful spoken language.

In conversation, Greek speakers differentiate between informal and formal address, and young people, older people, and rural folk almost always use informal forms, even with strangers. There are numerous words and phrases that are constantly used in Greek. The most common greeting is *yá sou* (YA soo), meaning "health to you," while *ti néa* (tee NEH-ah), meaning "what's new," is also used. If a Greek Cypriot wishes to express dismay, he or she will

The Greek alphabet used today was formed as far back as the Hellenistic period (300–100 BCE), and has heavily influenced the formation of other alphabets, including the Roman alphabet. There are twenty-four letters in the Greek alphabet, and thirteen main combinations or diphthongs.

Α,α (alpha)...... "a" as father

Β,β (beta)........ "v" as in vet

Γ,γ (gamma).... "y" as in yes

Δ,δ (delta)....... "the" as in then

Ε,ε (epsilon) .... "e" as in wet

Ζ,ζ (zeta)......... "z" as in zebra

Η,η (eta).......... "i" as in ski

Θ,θ (theta)....... "th" as in theme

Ι,ι (iota) .... "i" as in ski

Κ,κ (kappa)..... "g" as in get

Λ,λ (lambda).. "l" as in lolly

Μ,μ (mu)......... "m" as in man

Ν,ν (nu).......... "n" as in no

Ξ,ξ (xi)............. combination of "k" and "s," not found in English

Ο,ο (omikron) . "o" as in toad

Π,π (pi)............ "p" as in put
(sometimes like a "b" sound)

Ρ,ρ (rho).......... "r" as in terror

Σ,σ (sigma)...... "s" as in sat

Τ,τ (tau)........... "t" as in tight
(sometimes like a "d" sound)

Υ,υ (upsilon).... "i" as in ski

Φ,φ (phi)......... "f" as in fish

Χ,χ (hi) .... "ch" as in loch

Ψ,ψ (psi).......... "ps" as in lips

Ω,ω (omega).... "o" as in toad

say *pó-pó-pó* (POH-poh-poh); *όpα* (OH-pah) means "watch it" or "whoops"; and if Greek speakers want you to slow down and relax, they will say *sigá sigá* (see-GAH see-GAH).

THE TURKISH LANGUAGE

The Turkish language is a member of the Turkic family of languages, spoken by more than 170 million people living from the borders of China to the Balkans in southeastern Europe. Modern Turkish is a descendant of Ottoman Turkish, which itself descends from Old Anatolian. Over the centuries, Turkish has absorbed many Persian and Arabic words.

The Cypriot Turkish dialect is quite distinct from Standard Turkish used on the mainland. Turkish Cypriot usage is also very casual. Turks from Istanbul,

for example, consider Cypriot Turkish a slovenly dialect, while the Turkish Cypriots view Standard Turkish politeness and formality with amusement. Regional dialects also exist. Paphiot Turkish, spoken by Turkish Cypriot refugees from the Paphos district, shows the effects of a long cohabitation with Greek, containing many Greek words or variations of Greek words. However, the influx of mainland Turks and years of Turkish army occupation mean that mainland Turkish is becoming increasingly influential. Some peculiarities of the dialect are steadily being eroded. The influence of Turkish television has also contributed to the harmonizing of the two languages.

Turkish is notoriously difficult for Western European language speakers to learn, as the grammatical structure is unrelated to any Romance or Indo-European languages, and the word order is difficult. Turkish is characterized by a tendency to expand from an unchanging root word by attaching a vast array of suffixes, or word endings, to change the word's meaning. For example: *bilgi* (bihl-GEE) means "knowledge," while *bilgisiz* (bihl-gee-SIHZ) means "without knowledge," and *bilgisizlik* (bihl-gee-sihz-LIHK) means "lack of knowledge."

However, Turkish pronunciation is easier than Greek because the spelling is phonetic, and words are pronounced as they are spelled. Turkish vowels are usually short, and unlike Greek, there are no diphthongs, or vowel combinations—each vowel retains its individual sound. Stress is generally placed on the last syllable of a word, with the exception of place names. Typical Turkish greetings include *nasilsiniz* (nah-sihl-sih-NIHZ) and *ne haber* (neh hah-BER), both meaning "How are you?" Typical phrases include *bir dakika* (bih dah-kih-KAH), or "wait a minute," and *affedersiniz* (ahf-ehd-ehr-sih-NIHZ), meaning "sorry" or "I beg your pardon."

THE CYPRUS PRESS

The first Cypriot newspaper, published in both Greek and English, was circulated on August 29, 1878, under the name *Kypros* (Cyprus). The first Turkish Cypriot newspaper was circulated on July 11, 1889, under the name *Sadet* (Hope). Today, Cyprus has a relatively developed press with a large number of dailies, weeklies, and periodicals reflecting a wide range of ideologies and covering a variety of subjects. Perhaps surprisingly in comparison to many other countries, the

THE TURKISH ALPHABET

Until 1928, Turkish was written in the Arabic alphabet. Since the Arabic alphabet was deemed unsuitable for representing the sounds of Turkish, the language underwent radical reforms, with Arabic letters being replaced by the Latin alphabet. Today the Turkish alphabet has twenty-nine letters—eight vowels and twenty-one consonants.

a........... "a" as in man

b .... "b" as in bet

c........... "j" as in jam

ç........... "ch" as in church

d .... "d" as in dad

e........... "e" as in bed

f........... "f" as in fat

g........... "g" as in goat

ğ........... "y" as in yet

h .... "h" as in house

ı........... "i" as in cousin

i .... "ee" as in meet

j .... "s" as in treasure

k .... "k" as in key

l .... "l" as in land

m .... "m" as in mud

n .... "n" as in not

o .... "o" as in hot

ö .... "er" as in other

p .... "p" as in pot

r........... "r" as in ribbon

s........... "s" as in sing

ş........... "sh" as shall

t........... "t" as in take

u .... "u" as in push

ü .... "ew" as in yew

v........... "v" as in vast

y........... "y" as in yet

z........... "z" as in zebra

majority of the papers are still widely read and available in print. Cypriots are a highly literate, news-hungry people, as reflected in the many publications available on the island. This is partly a product of political organizations, such as trade unions and political parties, sponsoring publications on both sides of the divide. In the republic, popular daily papers in Greek include *Alithia* (Truth), a right-wing paper that supports the DISY party, and the moderate paper *Politis* (Politics). *O Phileleftheros* (The Liberal) is the oldest newspaper in Cyprus still in print and the one with the largest circulation. *Haravgi* (Dawn) is the mouthpiece of the communist AKEL party.

Popular English-language papers include the daily *Cyprus Mail* and the popular weekly paper *Cyprus Weekly*. Although the latter has become increasingly anti-Turkish, both are renowned for their news coverage. The *Blue*

The Maronites on Cyprus are descended from Christians who fled Lebanon and Syria in the eighth century CE. Their numbers now total approximately five thousand, with several hundred more in northern Cyprus. However, only nine hundred or so Maronites still speak their language on a regular basis, and most of those are elderly.

In a bid to prevent the language from dying out, Maronite communities have begun teaching the language to children and have compiled dictionaries.

Cypriot Maronite Arabic (CMA) has its roots in Aramaic, the language spoken by Jesus. Over the centuries, it has incorporated some words from Arabic, as well as from Greek, French, and Italian. Yet it remains an old-fashioned rural language, with no words for many modern technologies such as computers or mobile phones.

In 2008, the Cypriot government recognized CMA as a minority language and so encouraged attempts to keep the language going for generations to come. Travel rules have recently been relaxed, making it easier for Maronites in the north to cross the border and visit relatives. This has also helped more people learn the language that has defined their ancestors for centuries.

Many newspapers are on display in Nicosia.

Beret is an English-language newsletter for the UN forces posted in Cyprus. There are newspapers that cater to specific interests. For example, sports enthusiasts read *Athlitiko Vimo* (Sports Tribune), and those interested in business can read the *Financial Mirror*. There are also local publications such as the *Famagusta Gazette* and *Phonitis Pafou* (Voice of Paphos).

There are six daily newspapers and four weeklies published in northern Cyprus. The largest daily circulation newspapers are *Kibris*, and *Kibris Postasi*. These publications are of a general interest and include current news on local and international political events, crime, business, sports, opinions, weather forecasts, and some entertainment columns. *Cyprus Today*, founded in 1991, is the major English-language weekly newspaper in northern Cyprus. Another weekly title there is the *Cyprus Observer*, which is also distributed in Great Britain and has a more political standpoint.

BROADCAST MEDIA

The *Cyprus Mail* is the island's largest English-language daily newspaper.

The Cyprus Broadcasting Corporation (CyBC) began operations in 1957 and is Cyprus's public broadcasting service. Its four radio channels broadcast programs in Greek, English, Turkish, and Armenian. An international service also broadcasts in Greek, English, and Arabic, directed at the many overseas Cypriot communities who live all around the world.

More than twenty smaller radio stations operate across the island, and many can be listened to live online via the internet.

The CyBC runs three television stations—CyBC 1, CyBC 2, and RIK Sat, broadcasting in both Greek and Turkish. English-language and Greek programs from the mainland can be received via satellite, as can international satellite channels such as CNN and Star TV. The British Forces Broadcasting Service from the British military base at Akrotiri can be received throughout the island.

In northern Cyprus, Bayrak Radio and Television Corporation—or in Turkish, Bayrak Radyo Televizyon Kurumu (BRTK)—is the state-run broadcaster. From its station in Nicosia, BRTK broadcasts news, sports, arts, educational, cultural, entertainment, and other programs on both television and radio. The corporation oversees two television channels and several radio stations. Users can also access BRTK programs online.

INTERNET LINKS

https://www.media.net.gr/cyprus.php
Although named as a guide to Greek media, this contains a list of Cypriot radio and television stations with links to the homepages.

https://www.thenational.ae/world/europe/maronites-in-cyprus -try-to-revive-old-language-1.534650
This newspaper article describes attempts by Maronites in Cyprus to revive their old language.

http://www.onlinenewspapers.com/cyprus.htm
Here is a comprehensive list of links to all Cypriot newspapers.

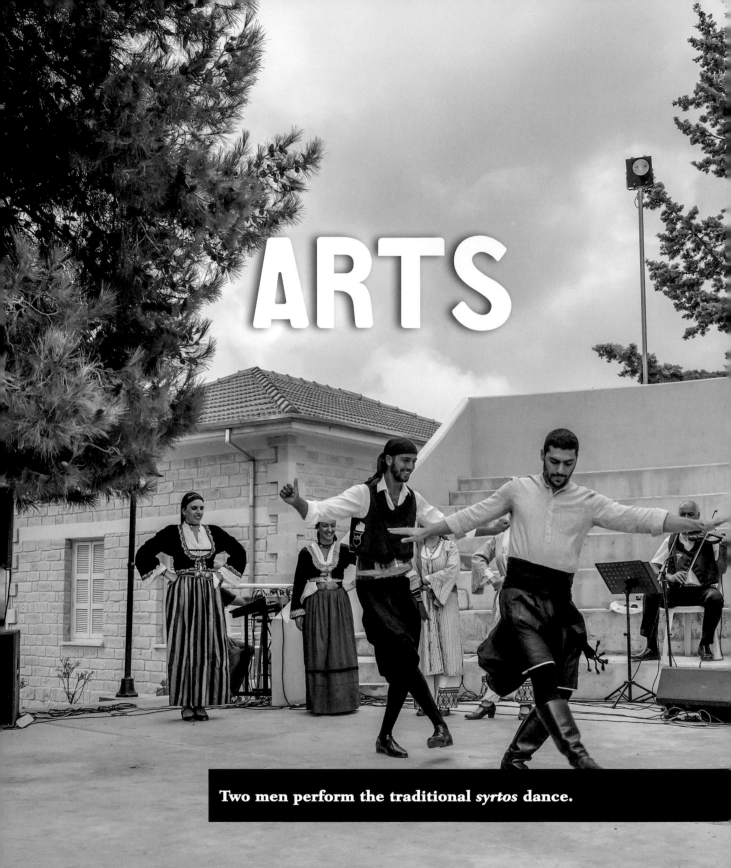

ARTS

Two men perform the traditional *syrtos* dance.

10

C YPRUS'S RICH HISTORY HAS SEEN many foreign influences. Greek and Turkish influences have been ongoing for centuries. Other cultures that have contributed to Cypriot arts and music range from the ancient (Roman, Persian, Byzantine, and Ottoman) to the more modern (British, European).

In many cultures, increased modernization means a decline in traditional art forms. However, folk music and dance remain highly influential and popular throughout Cyprus. This is largely due to the geographic isolation of the rural communities. Another factor that has helped has been the determination of governments in both the north and south to protect the island's heritage.

Archaeological projects and restoration endeavors are carried out to preserve the nation's many ancient and medieval sites. These attract a large number of tourists, which in turn contributes to the local economy and helps to support further restoration.

ANCIENT ARTIFACTS

Many of the best finds are in the island's various museums, including district museums in Larnaca, Limassol, and Paphos; the Pieredes Museum in Larnaca; and the Cyprus Museum in southern Nicosia. Unfortunately, only a small portion of Cyprus's ancient heritage has remained on the island. Many art objects were removed by European archaeologists in the

Many ancient artifacts have been found throughout Cyprus, like this amphora from 2500 BCE. Each object has its own story to tell of the island's rich history.

nineteenth and early twentieth centuries, and they are now found in museums all over the world.

Many figurines, some of very high quality, have survived from the Chalcolithic, or Copper Stone, period (3800—2800 BCE). The figures, usually made from picrolite, a soft, blue-green stone, include idols, female fertility symbols, and outstanding anthropomorphic figures shaped like a cross, or cruciforms. Copper items from the Bronze Age (2300—1050 BCE) confirm the island's reputation for metalwork. Many bronze items, especially jewelry and vessels, were discovered in the royal tombs at Salamis. Many beautiful handmade vases survive from this time. Terra-cotta figures, including toys and female fertility figures, date from the Archaic period (750—475 BCE). This period was also remarkable for its beautiful, embossed gold plaques and jewelry.

The Classical period (510—323 BCE) produced some large sculpture. The figurines wore Greek dress and had beards, reflecting the influence of Persia, as Persians at that time were known to have a love of long beards. The figures include an impressive representation of Aphrodite of Soli, which has become a popular symbol of Cyprus. Hellenistic art shows Athenian and Alexandrian influences, especially in the statues of local rulers and officials. The gold and jewelry of this period are magnificent. The Roman period between 27 BCE and 476 CE is most famous for mosaics. Excellent examples at Soli depict a waterfowl flanked by dolphins, and a swan enclosed by floral patterns. At Salamis, there are mosaics of the river god Evrotas and partial remnants of a battle scene. At Curium, fifth-century mosaics depict scenes from the Trojan War and Greek mythology, while others have animals and geometric shapes indicating growing Christian influences.

Ancient architecture includes the impressive sites of Curium, with its Roman-built temple of Apollo Hylates, and the temple of Aphrodite at Amathus. The most impressive ancient remains are at Salamis, north of Famagusta. Most of the ruins at Salamis date from the Hellenistic, Roman, and Byzantine periods. They include a gymnasium, baths, amphitheater, and 150 royal tombs from as far back as the seventh and eighth centuries BCE.

ARCHITECTURE

Lusignan rule left a considerable architectural legacy in Cyprus. The Lusignans were a noble French family that was powerful around the thirteenth and fourteenth centuries. In 1192, Guy of Lusignan received the island of Cyprus from King Richard I of England. In 1194, Guy's brother, Amalric II, succeeded him as king of Cyprus. Cyprus flourished under Lusignan rule, and Nicosia was a center of French medieval culture. In 1375, the last Lusignan king of Armenia was overthrown by the Mamluks, and in 1489, the Lusignan dynasty finally ended with Venice taking complete control of Cyprus. The Lusignans introduced fine Gothic architecture at a time when Western Europe was achieving its architectural zenith. One of these buildings is the Selimiye Mosque, a former cathedral, in the heart of old Nicosia. Originally built as Saint Sophia

This building is a prime example of the type of medieval architecture found in Famagusta.

Cathedral by French architects in 1209, its broad outline resembles some of the magnificent medieval cathedrals of France. Following the Ottoman occupation, the cathedral was converted to a mosque in 1571, and all Christian decorations were removed.

Famagusta is home to some of the most impressive medieval architecture in the Middle East. The famous painter Leonardo da Vinci is said to have been involved in the construction of its Venetian-style fortifications. The walls of Famagusta have a squat appearance—in some places they are 49 feet (15 m) tall and 26 feet (8 m) thick.

Cyprus has numerous examples of Renaissance military architecture. Some of the most elaborate include the castles at Kyrenia, Saint Hilarion, Buffavento, and Kantara. These are all situated in the Kyrenia Mountains. Saint Hilarion Castle, for example, was originally built by the Byzantines, mainly as a defense against Arab raiders and pirates. Nicosia's city walls contain a fascinating mixture of architecture that reflects the city's turbulent history. The walls were originally built by the Venetians in the sixteenth century. Although not high, they are extremely thick and were designed to allow cannons to be rolled along the ramparts.

Cyprus has many magnificent, isolated monasteries in the mountains. The ruins of Sourp Magar monastery are nestled amid the Kyrenia Mountains. Like many of the island's monasteries, it is a vestige of the Cypriot Church's powerful and wealthy past. Antiphonitis monastery, which contains many exquisite frescoes, is one of the most architecturally impressive religious buildings in Cyprus. Other well-known monasteries include the Stavrovouni monastery, perched on a rocky crag to the west of Larnaca. The monastery has a long and illustrious history. Founded by Saint Helena in 327 CE, the monastery is thought to have contained a fragment of the biblical True Cross. The monastery was burned in both Lusignan times and by the Ottomans. The present building dates from the nineteenth century.

The Kykkos monastery in the Troodos Mountains and the monastery of Ayios Chrysostomos on the southern slopes of the Kyrenia range were built in the eleventh century. They are classic examples of late Byzantine monastic architecture. The thirteenth-century abbey at Bellapais near Kyrenia boasts an impressive cloister, church, and magnificent refectory.

RELIGIOUS ARTWORK

Long-standing bastions of the Orthodox Christian religion, beautiful icons and frescoes have been painted in the churches and monasteries of Cyprus since Byzantine times. Icons are the principal religious art form of the Orthodox faith, transmitting to the faithful the glory of God. Depictions of biblical scenes and scenes from liturgical history, and images of the Virgin Mary, Jesus, and the apostles offer physical representations to inspire and direct the faith of worshippers. Icons are not merely works of art, but are imbued with religious significance and venerated by the faithful. Literally hundreds of churches all over the island are intricately decorated with religious reliefs and icons.

Magnificently colored frescoes fill many of Cyprus's churches, such as this one in the village of Lagoudera.

Icon painting began in the early Byzantine period, in the sixth century CE. Cyprus became a refuge for icon painters during the eighth and ninth centuries, when there were doctrinal disputes over whether it was appropriate to worship images. Because of this theological controversy, icons were destroyed in great numbers. Many of the more impressive church paintings found today are derived from the later Byzantine period, in the tenth through twelfth centuries. Many have faded beyond recognition, but some remarkable ones can still be found at Ayios Trypiotis in Nicosia, Ayios Lazaros in Larnaca, and the Apostolos Andreas monastery on the Karpas Peninsula. Some of the best icon painters in Europe practiced their art on the island, including the fourteenth-century master Philip Goul, who decorated the churches of Stavros tou Ayiasmati and Ayios Mamas at Louvaras, located high in the Troodos Mountains. Typical paintings depict scenes from the Bible, illustrating the lives of Jesus and the apostles. In the chapel of Ayios Mamas, impressive frescoes depict Jesus healing the sick and blind, the Last Supper, and John the Baptist. The most extensive collections of icons are held at the Icon Museum in Kyrenia and the Byzantine Museum in Nicosia.

Icon painting is highly stylized. The subject is captured with a perfect visage, frozen for eternity. Naturalistic representations are rare. Today, icon making continues in the monasteries, expressing religious fervor and devotion.

There is a vibrant contemporary art scene in Cyprus. This mural is one of many that line the streets of Nicosia.

CONTEMPORARY ART

Modern art did not develop in Cyprus until the beginning of the twentieth century, following trends in Europe. Since then, Cypriot artists have sought to capture the moods and nuances of the landscape. One of Cyprus's better-known painters and sculptors, Christoforos Savva (1924—1968), painted in an innovative post-Cubist style using sharp, magnificent colors. His most famous works are *Nude* (1957) and the abstract *Composition with Two Circles* (1967). Other well-known Cypriot artists include Stass Paraskos (1933—2014), who was influenced by the island's artistic and archaeological heritage; the constructivist Stelios Votsis (1929—2012); and the expressionist Vera Hadjida (b. 1936). Andreas Savvides (1930—2016) produced work that included monumental sculptures

REVITALIZING CONTEMPORARY CYPRIOT ART

The last few years have seen an exciting resurgence of modern art in Cyprus as many young artists have returned to the island. In 2017, Cyprus was rediscovering itself as a hub of contemporary art in the Mediterranean region.

Although Cyprus has a long and vibrant artistic history, it has not always been the ideal place for many artists to work. Until very recently, there were no fine art programs at universities on the island, and so budding artists would travel overseas, often to Britain, France, or Germany, to continue their studies. After graduating, many stayed in their newly adopted homes, where they found strong support networks for exhibiting and selling. As well as having a lack of educational programs in the arts, Cyprus also had one of the lesser developed markets. There were few successful art galleries, and even fewer survived the financial crisis. There seemed to be little reason to return to Cyprus as an artist.

That has changed, with many young artists, sculptors, and photographers now returning home and creating uniquely Cypriot creative spaces. They are working in collective spaces and are seeking to produce work that is affordable and that attracts a broader audience. These artists are seeking to create a strong local identity independent of outside European influences.

While politics, religion, and division continue to be influential themes, a lot of the younger artists are trying to break away from these, arguing that they do not want to be defined by events of forty years ago. Instead, they are drawing inspiration from aspects of modern Cypriot culture that they see as uniting rather than dividing people. Examples of these collaborative groups include Thkio Ppalies and Pick Nick, both in Nicosia.

and abstract compositions combining different materials. Sculptor Yorgos Kypris (b. 1954) was born in Nicosia but currently lives in Greece. He continues to produce work that is exhibited around the world. Since 2015, he has gained attention for his series of installations that have explored the connection between politics and religion, be it Orthodox Christianity or Islam. Ruzen Atakan (b. 1966) is the daughter of painter Ali Atakan. Her work has been widely exhibited, and she teaches in Nicosia at one of the island's only fine art programs.

Inspired by centuries of Greek and Roman literature, poetry remains extremely popular in Cyprus, perhaps more so than novels.

LITERARY ARTS

Although not widely known outside the island, Cyprus has a rich literary tradition, including a two-time nominee for the Nobel Prize for Literature. Poet Osman Türkay (1927—2001) wrote in his native Turkish and was nominated in 1988 and again in 1992. Other notable poets include Taner Baybars and Kyriakos Charalambides. Baybars moved to England in the 1950s. He wrote in English, using his own name and the pen name Timothy Bayliss. Charalambides writes in Greek and is considered one of Cyprus's most notable literary figures. In the field of novel writing, Andreas Koumi received critical acclaim in 2009 for his novel *The Cypriot*. Meanwhile, Armenian Cypriot Nora Nadjarian has attracted praise and controversy for her poetry and short stories, which include *Cleft in Twain* and *Girl, Wolf, Bones*. Cyprus has also served as inspiration for writers from elsewhere. British writer Lawrence Durrell spent several years on the island in the 1950s. *Bitter Lemons* is a memoir of his time in Cyprus.

FOLK ARTS AND CRAFTS

Folk art is still alive and well in Cyprus, and weaving and lacework are still a part of the lives of many Cypriot women, especially in the villages. It has been argued that Cypriot arts and crafts have their origin in the need of young women to be provided with a dowry. Men would craft objects from copper, gourds, and wood. Mothers and daughters would also produce great quantities of embroidered linen for the bride's dowry, to provide bed sheets, pillowcases, furniture coverings, towels, and floor covers. Today, the picturesque village of Lefkara, in the foothills of the Troodos Mountains west of Larnaca, is the center of this craft tradition, famous for its lace embroidery and silver creations.

Although Lefkara's lace industry prospers, the same cannot be said for other cottage industries in Cyprus. High-quality pottery and ceramics, for example, have been produced in Cyprus for many centuries, but producers have found themselves unable to compete internationally. In the past, *pitharia* (PIH-thah-ree-ah), containers 3 feet (about 1 meter) in diameter and made by highly regarded craftsmen, were produced for storing olive oil, olives, and wine. Today, they are often used to hold flowers in gardens. Small pottery, including glazed vases, figurines, bowls, and pitchers, is the specialty of the Paphos district. These are often decorated with floral patterns or geometric designs reminiscent of their ancient counterparts. Gourd flasks have also been made for centuries, although they are not often used today. Wickerwork and basketry are also common.

TRADITIONAL MUSIC

In Cyprus, music and dance are traditionally the most popular art forms. Today, traditional forms play alongside more modern pop music, with some artists exploring how to fuse the two. Most Cypriot boys and girls learn to dance both traditional and modern variations of dances at school. Some purists believe that although dance classes in school are useful to ensure a wide knowledge of Cypriot dance, the classes also limit the spontaneity of the performers by encouraging uniformity of movement.

An elderly woman works on traditional handicrafts in Cyprus.

Dances are usually performed on special occasions, such as at weddings, or on festival days. In the past, men would dance not only on festive occasions, but also in coffeehouses in the evening, or even on the threshing floor. Today, the occasions for dancing are more restricted. There are many kinds of Cypriot dances, most of which can be performed by both men and women. Traditionally, men danced with men, and women with women. The only exception was when the bride danced with the groom at a wedding party. Mixed dancing, although once frowned upon by traditionalists, is now widespread and has added a new degree of vitality and spontaneity to Cypriot dance.

Stylistically, men's dances were usually more lively, while women's dances were more delicate and restrained. The best-known dance is the *kartchilamas* (gar-chee-LAH-mahs), performed by pairs of male and female dancers. Often this will form the foundation for a much broader suite, rounded off with more complicated dances such as the *syrtos* (SEE-tohs) and *mandra* (MAHN-drah). The *syrtos* is a particularly popular dance at social gatherings, such as weddings. The *kartchilamas*, a very lively dance, offers the men the opportunity to compete

Currently, one of the most popular musical acts from Cyprus is Monsieur Doumani. The three-person band got its start in Nicosia in 2011 and quickly gathered a large following both at home and on the international world music scene. They have performed at a number of major festivals around the world.

Monsieur Doumani's music combines traditional Cypriot sounds and instruments with more modern musical styles and poetry. Their lyrics often contain commentary about contemporary social and political events, such as the recent financial crisis and the collapse of the Greek banks.

The band uses a variety of instruments, both modern and traditional. These include multiple wind instruments, the guitar, and the tzouras *(TZOW-ras), which is a type of lute with either six or eight strings.*

Monsieur Doumani released their third album in February 2018, and it quickly rose to the top of the Transglobal World Music Chart.

with each other and demonstrate their strength, while the women's dances tend to stress restraint and grace. Stamping feet on one spot is a typical feature of the *kartchilamas* and the *syrtos*. The *dhrepanin* (threh-PAH-neen), or "sickle dance," has an agricultural theme, where the male dancers cut imaginary swathes in the air and around their bodies as they mow the harvest. This dance is particularly popular at the Kataklismós festival, and it allows male dancers to express themselves energetically. In the women's dances, the woman stays in one spot, and much of the movement is in the positioning of the arms and the turning of the body.

Cypriots take great pride in their traditional folk songs. Love songs, working songs, children's rhymes, humorous songs, wedding songs, laments, and political rhymes are all part of the Cypriot canon. A popular musical form with ancient origins is the *kalamatianos* (gar-LAH-mah-tee-ah-nohs), which is paired with a dance of the same name.

In its purest and most traditional form, music is played on a shepherd's flute, or *auloi* (ow-LOH-ee). The violin and flute are used to accompany dance performances. Another traditional instrument is the *laoudo* (LAH-oo-doh), or long-necked flute. Turkish traditional instruments include the *zorna* (zoh-NAH), a kind of oboe; the *davul* (dah-VUHL), a two-headed drum; and the *kasat* (kah-SAHT), or small finger cymbals. As seen in the example of the popular band Monsieur Doumani, modern musicians frequently blend traditional musical styles and instruments with more modern counterparts. .

A man plays a traditional handcrafted shepherd's flute in Nicosia.

INTERNET LINKS

http://www.kypros.org/Cyprus/dance.html
This looks at the variety of Cypriot folk dances and the types of movement in each form.

http://www.kypros.org/CyprusPanel/cyprus/arts.html
Here is a condensed look at arts in Cyprus from some of the earliest sculptures to more recent art and literature festivals.

http://www.visitcyprus.com/index.php/en/discovercyprus/culture -religion/other-sites-of-interest/item/577-traditional-handicrafts
Cyprus has a wide range of traditional handicrafts that are studied in this article. Among those included are stoneware, lacework, copperware, and basketry.

LEISURE

Cyprus evokes many images of lush beaches, such as this one at Paphos.

11

CYPRUS OFTEN CONJURES UP IMAGES of a lush Mediterranean island with beautiful beaches, azure blue waters, and charming little villages. These villages are filled with tavernas—cafés or small restaurants—and people relaxing as they eat, drink, and enjoy life. In many ways, this is not far from reality. The people of Cyprus value their leisure time and enjoy relaxing outdoors with good conversation and good food. Men gather to play backgammon, an ancient board game, or to go hunting. Along the coast, people enjoy water sports and lounging on the beach. Other popular outdoor pursuits include hiking, playing sports, and golf. Visitors flock to the island in search of that same relaxed lifestyle in beautiful surroundings.

There is more to Cyprus for tourists than beaches. There are also opportunities for hiking and even skiing in winter.

ENJOYING THE OUTDOORS

Cyprus's warm climate makes it an ideal location for outdoor activities. Family picnics on Sundays or festival days are popular. The whole family will travel to the coast or the countryside and eat kebabs in the shade of an olive tree. The low temperatures in the Troodos Mountains make the area an ideal place to relax.

Nature trails have been marked recently along the coast and in the mountains. Hikers, often tourists, can easily follow signs that give details about the local flora and fauna in Greek and English.

Cyprus boasts of one leisure activity that is considered exotic in the Middle East—skiing. There is a ski resort on the northeastern face of Mount Olympus in the Troodos Mountains. It is open from January to early April. An international ski event—the Troodos International FIS Ski Race—which attracts top skiers from around the world, is held in February or March.

The hunting of small game and birds has traditionally been popular in Cyprus. In the 1970s, it was estimated that as many as ten million birds were killed each year in

Whatever the weather, Cypriots enjoy spending time outdoors.

Cyprus—more than fifteen birds for every man, woman, and child on the island! Although this number has since decreased, and some species have become protected in nature reserves, hunting remains popular. The hills around the village of Dipkarpas on the Karpas Peninsula are considered the best spot on the island for hunting birds. In the hunting season, which lasts from November to January, the sport is so popular that men travel from Morphou, which is at the other end of the island, to participate. The catch is normally taken home and cooked. Hares and rabbits are also hunted. Since joining the EU in 2004, Cyprus has come under pressure to reinforce its bird protection laws. Although these bird protection laws are in place, illegal bird hunting continues to occur, with an estimated 3.2 million birds killed illegally every year.

BEAUTIFUL BEACHES

Cyprus adheres to the "Blue Flag Program," which promotes clean and environmentally friendly beaches. There are several Blue Flag beaches located around the southern coastline. In the north, there are some outstanding, secluded coves and bays for swimming. The stretch of Famagusta Bay, for example, is considered one of the finest beaches in the Mediterranean. There are also many small beaches along the northern coast to the west and east of Kyrenia. Popular beaches include

Tourists enjoy the Mediterranean weather and the scenery by touring sea caves.

those at Lara Bay and Alakati. The former is famous as a breeding ground for loggerhead turtles and a vital environmental resource—during the breeding season, the beach is reserved for turtles. Other beaches along the northern coast are used by the Turkish Cypriots, and on the weekends they become crowded with families having barbecues and enjoying the sea air. The southern coastline of the Karpas Peninsula has some of the island's most beautiful, inaccessible, and unspoiled beaches. Here, the Nangomí (also called Golden) Beach, which runs for 3 miles (4.8 km), is probably the best—and cleanest— beach on the entire island, with not a soft drink bottle or taverna in sight.

Many of the tourist beaches in the south have been artificially created, especially around Limassol and Paphos, where the shore has been improved with sand brought from elsewhere. Other good beaches include Governor's Beach, 20 miles (32 km) east of Limassol; and Pissouri Beach, west of the British base at Akrotiri. While the beaches around Ayia Napa provide some good stretches of sand, every inch is filled by the many thousands of tourists who visit the area. Although the beaches in the south are of a poorer quality, they tend to have more facilities, with water sports, beachside tavernas, drink vendors, beach furniture, and children's playgrounds all provided. Throughout the south, it is difficult to find the seclusion that defines the north. The exception is the isolated and often off-limits Akamas Peninsula, where a number of excellent unspoiled beaches remain, protected by British military rights to practice bombing and firing.

Illegal bird hunting is a huge problem in Cyprus, with millions trapped or killed each year. Conservationists are working with the government to try to stop the practice.

The island's huge tourist industry has led to an explosion of water and beach sports, including windsurfing, waterskiing, speed boating, sailing, jet skiing, scuba diving, and parasailing. Some beaches even have bungee-jumping facilities. These activities are based around the hotels and are most popular with tourists and expatriates. The capes near Paphos, Ayia Napa, and Protaras are the most popular spots for windsurfing, while sailing is popular in the bays off Larnaca and Limassol. Diving is popular in waters all around the island, thanks to the crystal-clear water and rocky coastline. Submarine cliffs and valleys, coral, and exotic sea life provide plenty of underwater attractions for divers.

URBAN NIGHTLIFE

Traditionally, Cypriots of all ages spend their time chatting over food and drinks for the whole evening in their favorite taverna or restaurant. Although Cypriots tend to avoid the resort areas such as Ayia Napa, many young Cypriots enjoy the nightlife of Nicosia, Limassol, and Paphos. The rapid expansion of the island's tourist scene has led to an explosion of clubs, bars, and restaurants in the main tourist areas. Nightclubs, bars, and pubs have only been recently introduced to Cyprus. The EU decision in 2010 to ban smoking inside bars

Turkish baths can be found in many parts of the Middle East and eastern Mediterranean, and in many of the cities of Cyprus. One of the largest and best known, the Büyük Hamam, which means "the Grand Baths," lies in northern Nicosia. It provides traditional Turkish baths. Fridays are reserved for women, but all other days are for men only. The treatment includes an exposure to warm air, then steam, followed by a massage, and finally a cold shower. Most baths have separate washrooms and soaking pools.

Bathers spend many happy hours sweating in the hot rooms, followed by washing with a camel-hair glove, or perhaps a vigorous massage by a masseur. The bath is considered an excellent way to lose weight, cleanse the skin, and generally relax the mind and body. Those who believe in the medicinal qualities of the Turkish bath try to visit as often as possible—at least once a month, or even once a week.

and clubs proved unpopular with older people, and so many clubs in the larger, more touristy areas tend to be patronized by younger Cypriots and vacationers. Away from the more heavily populated areas, bars continue to attract smokers, regardless of local regulations.

Movies are also popular in Cyprus, especially international and American ones. These films usually have Greek or Turkish subtitles, depending on which side of the border they are shown. Big movie theaters pack in moviegoers in Nicosia, Larnaca, and Limassol. The Rialto in Limassol dates back to the 1930s and hosts some of Cyprus's most prestigious film festivals and theatrical events. Elsewhere in Limassol, Sto Perama attracts an impressive roster of Greek acts.

A taxi waits for passengers in the early morning, as the evening's nightlife ends.

After an evening of theater, film, or music, café bars offer an eclectic meeting place well into the early morning hours. Larnaca's 1900 Art Café has a menu that features more than one hundred wines, beers, and whiskies, and walls covered in old movie posters. In Nicosia's old town, Kala Kathoumena is considered the place to hang out and chat for hours.

A NATION OF SPORTS FANS

Cyprus is a nation of keen sports fans, and the island, although small, has had some notable recent successes.

As in most of Europe, soccer is the most popular sport, both to play and to watch. Here, players from Cyprus (*right*) play Norway (*left*).

Soccer remains the most popular sport on the island, both north and south of the divide, and it attracts more spectators than any other sport. Recently, several teams have advanced to the group stage of the UEFA Champions League, the highest club-level competition in Europe. In 2012, APOEL FC became the first Cypriot team to reach the quarterfinals of the UEFA Champions League.

Cypriots also like tennis, both as players and spectators, and courts in the hotels and public areas of the towns in the south are always booked. A well-known Greek Cypriot tennis player is Markos Baghdatis, who advanced to the Australian Open final and the Wimbledon semifinals in 2006. In that same year, he was ranked number eight in the world. The sport remains highly popular, although Cypriots still eagerly await someone to follow in Baghdatis's footsteps.

Although Cyprus is not at the forefront of world athletics, the island has strong athletic traditions, stretching back to the time of the ancient Greeks. Cypriots are also thought to have participated in the earliest Olympic games. With the Ottoman occupation and arrival of the Turks, weightlifting was encouraged as the national sport. Cyprus received its first Olympic medal in 2012 when Pavlos Kontides took silver in the men's laser class sailing event.

Every September, the Cyprus Car Rally attracts entries from many world-class championship drivers. The winding tracks and rugged landscape offer competitors a tough test of their driving abilities. Another very popular sport is basketball.

Although soccer is very popular on both sides of the divide, the most popular sports in northern Cyprus by number of participants are, surprisingly, tae kwon do and karate.

BASKETBALL

Football, or soccer, may be the most popular sport in Cyprus, but basketball comes a close second. A large majority of the population likes to follow the sport or play it themselves.

The Cyprus Basketball Federation (CBF) was founded in 1966. In 1974, it became a full member of the International Basketball Federation (FIBA). During this early period, the most popular teams were Digenis Akritas Morphou (based in Morphou) and PAEEK (in Kyrenia). However, the Turkish invasion in 1974 saw both teams expelled from their hometowns. For the next thirteen years, basketball, like many other sports, struggled to cope with economic problems and lack of development. But things began to improve again in 1987 when Greece won the Eurobasket tournament. Their success saw a revitalized interest in the sport, and more companies began to invest in building teams. Some foreign players came to Cyprus to play, and soon fans were flocking to games.

In the twenty-first century, Cypriot basketball teams have improved on the international level. In 2008, AEL Limassol finished third in the FIBA Eurocup.

INTERNET LINKS

http://www.cyprusalive.com/en/sports-in-cyprus
This article outlines some of the favorite sports in Cyprus and the most popular teams.

http://www.visitcyprus.com/index.php/en
The homepage for the Cyprus Tourism Organization contains links to information about where to go and what to do if planning a trip to the island.

FESTIVALS

Dancers take part in a carnival parade in Limassol.

12

T HE ORTHODOX CHURCH IS AT THE center of family and community life in much of the Republic of Cyprus. Therefore, religious holidays and festivals dominate the calendar, much more so than in many non-Orthodox Christian countries. Some festivals also have links to earlier pagan celebrations. As tourism has become a more important part of the Cypriot economy, a number of festivals have developed to attract visitors. Wine festivals in key resort areas are one such example.

Northern Cyprus, despite its links to Islam, is much more secular than many Muslim nations. While some festivals are religious in nature, there are just as many that are linked to local events and Turkish history.

Throughout Cyprus, one can find numerous small local festivals. A village may celebrate a local saint and this becomes a large feast, with people returning home to join in the festivities, which may include food, drink, music, dancing, and parades.

RELIGIOUS FESTIVALS FOR GREEK CYPRIOTS

Among Greek Cypriots, the Orthodox religion plays a central role in the history, identity, and life of the community. Many age-old pagan festivals

Many festivals in Cyprus are religious in nature, but that doesn't mean there isn't a large amount of dancing and feasting.

In Kathikas, this Good Friday celebration includes a reenactment of the crucifixion.

Anthestiriya, a festival to celebrate spring, takes place every May in Limassol with huge flower parades.

have over the centuries been given an Orthodox interpretation, while maintaining notable pagan elements. New Year's Day, for example, is celebrated with the Feast of Ayios Vasílios, or Saint Basil (329—379), one of the spiritual fathers of the Orthodox Church who is respected throughout the Orthodox world. Saint Basil was once considered the Cypriot equivalent of Santa Claus. Historically, gifts were exchanged on this day rather than Christmas. However, as outside influences have become more widespread, this is no longer the case, and the tradition has died out in many areas.

The Epiphany on January 6 marks the baptism of Christ in the River Jordan. It is called Fóta (FOH-tah) by Cypriots, meaning "illumination." On this day, holy water fonts in churches are blessed to banish the evil spirits that are said to have lurked on Earth since Christmas. The festival is also marked by the baking of doughnuts. It is customary to throw the first doughnut on the roof of the house to scare away any lingering evil spirits. In seaside towns, the celebration reaches a finale when the local bishop throws a crucifix far out into the water and young men swim for the honor of recovering it. March 25 fulfills the dual function of celebrating Greek Independence Day and the Feast of the Annunciation.

Easter is the most important celebration in the Greek Orthodox calendar. Many festivals are linked to the Easter festivities. Green Monday, the last Monday before Lent begins, is celebrated in late February or early March. The day is also known as Clean Monday. A national public holiday, Green Monday allows families and communities to celebrate before the beginning of Lent. They gather outdoors and fly kites before feasting on locally caught seafood,

The Festival of the Flood, or Kataklismós (kaht-ah-klees-MOHS), is unique to Cyprus and is celebrated seven weeks after Easter. Elsewhere in the Orthodox world it is merely Pentecost, but in Cyprus it becomes a celebration that can last anywhere from seven to ten days, especially in coastal towns.

The festival marks Pentecost and the Holy Spirit coming down to the apostles. However, in Cyprus the date also marks the Old Testament story of the great flood, and Noah saving mankind by building the ark. Other roots of the traditional Kataklismós include a pagan festival dedicated to water and ancient Greek festivals to honor Aphrodite and Adonis. These have all combined into one giant celebration.

Coastal towns typically throw the biggest festivals of the flood. There is traditional dancing and music, as well as games, parties, food stalls, and concerts late into the night. Boat races and swimming competitions are also part of the watery theme.

On Monday (known as Whit Monday in some church calendars), festivalgoers are purified with water. People splash each other all day long. A bishop will wade into the sea to throw a cross into the water, and divers will all seek to retrieve it. Farther inland, people now rely on water guns or on a traditional type of pump made with reeds for the occasion.

olives, fruits, and cakes. Dancing and music also feature in the festivities. After Green Monday, Easter observances begin with Lenten fasting for a full forty days.

Orthodox Good Friday is marked by processions through the villages led by a coffin containing a figure of Christ. The difference in timing between Western and Eastern churches in celebrating Easter can range from the same day to up to four weeks. Village women prepare elaborate floral decorations for the funeral bier. Every icon is draped in black cloth to mark the crucifixion. On

There are many
festivals in
northern Cyprus,
celebrating music
and food harvests.

Saturday night, huge bonfires are lit, and villagers gather in the local church to celebrate Jesus Christ's resurrection. Everyone holds a candle, while children hold sparklers. At midnight, the priest announces Christ's resurrection and eternal life for all believers. The priest passes around a lighted flame, which is handed from worshipper to worshipper. The Lenten fast is broken immediately after the service, with the eating of egg and lemon soup and the cracking of dyed eggs. On Good Friday, preparations get under way for the baking of special holiday cakes, called *flaoúnes* (flah-OON-ehs), a pastry filled with egg, cheese, and raisins. These are then enjoyed on Easter Sunday as part of the celebrations.

The Assumption of the Virgin, on August 15, marks the rise to heaven of the Virgin Mary and is an important Orthodox festival. The day is celebrated with fairs in many villages and monasteries. Christmas is a far less important holiday in the Orthodox Church, and it is relatively subdued in Cyprus. Western-style commercialization has changed Christmas celebrations in recent years, and it is now more common to give and receive presents. The most durable traditional custom is the singing of carols—children go door-to-door, singing, accompanied by a triangle.

Other Orthodox festivals are also celebrated—Saint Anthony's Day, which honors the Egyptian father of the monastic life, is marked in Nicosia and Limassol on January 17, while Saint George's Day, on April 23, is celebrated almost everywhere on the island. Apart from island-wide Orthodox festivals, many other celebrations are held locally throughout Cyprus, to honor the local patron saint or holy figure of a monastery. These include the Erection of the Holy Cross at the Stavrovouni monastery in Larnaca on September 14, and the celebration of Saints Peter and Paul in Paphos on June 29, which is attended by the archbishop and other bishops of the island. Saint Neophytos's Day, on January 24, honors the Cypriot religious figure and is celebrated with a massive procession that ends at the famous hermit's cave north of Paphos.

FESTIVALS IN THE MUSLIM CALENDAR

In northern Cyprus all major Islamic festivals are celebrated according to the lunar calendar, meaning that the festival recedes by eleven days each

LAND OF MIRACLES

On Assumption Day (August 15) and Saint Andrew's Day (November 30), many pilgrims—both Christians and Muslims—pay a visit to the Apostolos Andreas monastery (monastery of Saint Andrew), near the tip of the Karpas Peninsula. The monastery has a reputation as the "Lourdes" of Cyprus, where pilgrims seek cures for their afflictions. This reputation stems from a visit to the spot made by the apostle Saint Andrew, the great miracle worker and protector of travelers. He is thought to have stopped here to fetch water while on a trip to preach Christianity in Greece. After restoring the sight of the one-eyed captain of his ship with the local water, Saint Andrew is said to have converted and baptized the crew. As a result, a chapel was built in the fifteenth century at the tiny spring in a nearby rock grotto thought to have healing powers. For many years, it was rumored that the site could heal blindness, deafness, and illnesses of all kinds.

year. Seker Bayrami (sheh-kehr bay-rah-MIH), meaning "the sugar festival," because of the great amount of sweets eaten at this time, is celebrated at the end of the fasting month, Ramadan. This three-day holiday, known elsewhere as Eid al-Fitr, is commonly celebrated with a family get-together and the distribution of sweets and presents to the children. Kurban Bayrami (kehr-bahn bay-rah-MIH), the Feast of the Sacrifice (also called Eid al-Adha), commemorates Abraham's willingness to sacrifice his son, and usually occurs two months after Seker Bayrami. Traditionally, families sacrifice a sheep or chicken, which is then eaten at a large family gathering. Kurban Bayrami is usually a four-day national holiday, the longest of the year. The Muslim new year and Mevlúd (mehv-LUHD), or the birth of the Prophet Muhammad, are also celebrated.

Turkish delight is eaten during Seker Bayrami.

SECULAR FESTIVALS

The Republic of Cyprus hosts many nonreligious festivals, especially in the summer. Although some of these celebrations have a traditional or pagan origin, many of them have been revamped and promoted by the tourist authorities to attract ever-increasing numbers of visitors. The most important city festival in Cyprus is the Limassol Wine Festival, held for around ten days every September. The city's municipal gardens become the site for contemporary merrymaking, where visitors pay an entrance fee that entitles them to sample any of the wines available and attend all the musical and theatrical activities. All the island's wineries take part.

Not all festivals are religious. Some are secular and can be enjoyed by children of all backgrounds.

The Street Life Festival, held at the end of April in Limassol, attracts more than twenty thousand visitors. Graffiti artists from around the world flock to the old town to decorate the sidewalks and walls, filling the city with a temporary boost of contemporary color. Also at the festival are street performers, a huge market, and live music.

In May, virtually every town holds a flower festival. The festivities include colorful processions through the streets and competitions for the best flower arrangements. Harvest festivals are also a common feature in some of the larger villages on the island. The whole district will celebrate with singing, feasting, and dancing in the village square.

The more tourist-oriented International Festival of Ancient Greek Drama is staged during the summer months at ancient ruins around the island, including the Paphos Ancient Odeon and the Curium Ancient Theater. Paphos also organizes the popular Paphos Carnival. In Larnaca, the annual Festival of Classical Music takes place every April. Limassol hosts an International Arts Festival in June and July.

On October 1, Cyprus's Independence Day is celebrated to mark the island's independence, while Greek Independence Day is celebrated on March 25, in solidarity with their brethren on the mainland.

TURKISH HOLIDAYS

In the north, many official holidays have been imported from the Turkish mainland. However, there are still some impressive local festivals, particularly those celebrating local culture and local food. In March, people flock to the villages near Lapta to ride their bikes among the fields of tulips as part of the Tepebasi Tulip Festival. May and June are filled with cultural events such as the Famagusta Art and Cultural Festival, the Lapta Tourism Festival (hosted by the local expatriate community), and the Iskele International Folk Dance Festival. Also in June, the village of Lefke celebrates its walnut harvest, while in August people gather to enjoy and celebrate their beloved *halloumi* (hah-LOO-mih) cheese. The Gecitkale Halloumi Festival doesn't just involve cheese and cooking with it; the event also includes photography contests and fashion parades. Harvest festivals in the villages on the Mesaoria Plain are probably the liveliest events, celebrated to mark the harvesting of the orange, strawberry, and watermelon crops.

INTERNET LINKS

https://www.justlanded.com/english/Cyprus/Cyprus-Guide/ Culture/Festivals-in-Cyprus
Here you can find information about a few of the more notable religious and cultural festivals in Cyprus.

https://www.myguidecyprus.com/usefulinfo/important-days-and -festivals-in-cyprus
This website lists key holidays and festival days in the Cyprus calendar.

FOOD

This table is laid out for a feast, complete with many traditional foods, such as feta cheese and raki.

13

A S WOULD BE EXPECTED FOR A Mediterranean island with close ties to the land and the sea, the Cypriot diet focuses on hearty yet simple meals consisting of local produce. Historical influences are also found. Geographic proximity to the Middle East and southern Europe has made its mark on Cypriot food. There are also some influences from the period of British rule.

Obviously, the strongest influences are Greece and Turkey. Both countries have strong culinary traditions. A typical meal might include locally caught seafood, meat (lamb or chicken are the most popular options), bread, vegetables, olives, and salad. The dinner table is more than just a place to eat. It is a place to socialize, to enjoy company and conversation, and to celebrate the day's work.

GREEK CYPRIOT CUISINE

Traditionally, Cypriots ate a simple rural diet of bread, olives, and yogurt, accompanied by cheese, tomatoes, and cucumbers. The dish was drizzled with salt, olive oil, and lemon. Today, Cyprus's newfound wealth has resulted in a richer, more varied diet for most Cypriots.

Meat is usually the highlight of any Greek Cypriot meal. Game, including duck, pigeon, quail, and rabbit, is the favorite, but it is only

Olives and bread are an essential part of many Cypriot meals.

eaten on special occasions. Souvlaki (soov-LAH-kee), or lamb roasted on a spit, often forms the culinary focus of any big gathering. *Kleftikó* (glehf-tee-KOH), which is lamb or goat roasted with an assortment of vegetables in an outdoor oven, is probably the closest thing to a national dish on the island. Every farmhouse and many other houses will have an outdoor oven for the preparation of this dish. Sausages, another popular choice, come in various forms—*sheftalia* (shehf-TAHL-yah) is grilled sausage made from ground meat, while *pastourmas* (past-oor-MAHS) is a garlic sausage made from pork. Fried meatballs, or *keftedes* (kehf-TEH-dehs), complete the typical Cypriot meat selection.

Bread is an essential part of the Cypriot meal and is always first served as a complement to the expected courses. The pita (PEE-tah)—a flat, crescent-shaped, hollow bread—is most often eaten filled with salad or vegetables and souvlaki. Vegetable dishes are usually either grilled or fried in oil, garnished with herbs, and mixed with a little tomato and olive oil. Favorites include stuffed or plain *kolokithakia* (koh-loh-kee-THA-kyah), or squash, *koukia* (koo-KYAH), or broad beans, and *koupepia* (koo-PEH-pyah), or vine leaves filled with rice and formed into rolls. *Moussakas* (moo-sah-KAHS)—layered ground beef, potatoes, and slices of eggplant, baked in a white sauce with a cheese topping—is popular.

Cyprus has a number of pureed dips that can be eaten either with a full meal or as a snack, usually with pita bread. These include hummus, or chickpeas pureed and mixed with garlic and lemon; *taramas*, a pink fish-roe pâté made with potato puree, lemon, and onions; *talatoúra* (tah-lah-TOO-rah), a yogurt, cucumber, and herb dip that is very cooling and especially good with spicy meat dishes; and tahini, or sesame seed paste.

Although Cypriots are less inclined to eat snacks compared to their mainland Greek and Turkish counterparts, baked tidbits are popular. In the south, these include *kolokótes* (koh-loh-KOH-tehs), a triangular pastry stuffed with pumpkin, cracked wheat, and raisins; *takhino pita* (tah-chee-NOH-pee-tah), a pastry with sesame paste; and *eliópitta* (ehl-YOH-pee-tah), an olive turnover.

Cypriots love to share a mixture of as many assorted dishes as possible. This style of dining is known as meze *(meh-ZEE), meaning "mixture."* Meze *is the most popular way of entertaining in the home and is a feature of every restaurant and tavern menu.* Meze *usually includes a little of everything that is in the kitchen that day. In this way, it provides an excellent introduction to Cypriot cooking. A typical* meze *will usually include fried or grilled fish,* keftedes, *sheftalia, pastourmas, hirómeri (hee-ROH-meh-ree) or cured local ham, calamari (fried squid rings),* taramas *(tah-rah-MAHS), hummus, tahini, Greek salad, beans, pickled cauliflower, olives, any number of vegetable dishes, and great quantities of bread. Often, a few Cypriot specialties will be included, in particular* halloumi, *a rubbery cheese that is often served grilled or just eaten simply with bread and salad. It tastes especially good when fried. The great quantity of food and the vast array of tastes represent a test of appetite and endurance for even the most enthusiastic diner. This, more than any reason, is why Cypriots linger so long over their meals. The whole meal will be washed down with plenty of wine or beer.*

TURKISH FOOD

Halloumi cheese from Cyprus is made with a mixture of goat and sheep milk, and is often eaten grilled.

Turkish Cypriot cuisine owes its heritage to a mixture of Middle Eastern and southern European influences. Although it has the same fundamental characteristics as Greek Cypriot food, the food in the north has become increasingly influenced by mainland tastes since the partition. As in the republic, *meze* is extremely popular. Other more typical Turkish dishes include *yalanci dolma* (yah-lahn-CHI dohl-MAH), similar to *koupepia*, where vine leaves are stuffed with rice, onions, and tomatoes; *musakka* (moo-sah-KAH), similar to the Greek Cypriot dish; and *lazböregi* (lahz-behr-reh-YEH), or meat-filled crepes topped with yogurt. Turkish kebabs come in many varieties, including

Turkish food combines Middle Eastern and European influences. Lamb and seafood are popular choices.

the ubiquitous shish kebab, or marinated lamb skewered and grilled over charcoal; and the *köfte* (kehrf-TEH), or spiced meatballs. Seafood is also popular. Fresh lobster, crab, mussels, squid, rock bream, and sea bass can be found in the north, although they are expensive.

Salads and vegetable dishes typically include tomatoes, eggplant, red onions, cucumbers, peppers, olives, and radishes. *Fasulye piyaz* (fahs-uhl-YEH pih-YAHZ), a green bean salad topped with olives and hard-boiled eggs, is a common accompaniment to meals or as part of a *meze*. The curiously named *imam bayaldi* (ih-MAHM bah-yahl-DIH), meaning "the imam fainted," is a traditional dish of baked eggplant cut in strips and stuffed with onions, garlic, and tomatoes. Street vendors sell *börek* (behr-EHK), a rich, flaky pastry containing bits of meat or cheese. Homemade and sold on the street, *börek* is the pride of Turkish Cypriot cuisine.

DESSERTS

Cypriot desserts tend to be extremely sweet and are usually made with local fruit, honey, syrup, and pastry. *Soudzoúkou* (sood-ZOO-koo), a confection of almonds strung together and dipped in grape molasses and rosewater, is sold everywhere. *Baklavas* (pah-klah-VAHS) is the classic Cypriot sweet, made of filo pastry layers alternating with honey and nuts. *Daktila* (dahk-tee-LAH), a finger-shaped strudel pastry filled with cinnamon and dipped in syrup, is also common. *Halvas* (hahl-VAHS) is a sweet made from a grainy paste of semolina or tahini, while *loukoumades* (loo-koo-MAH-dehs) consists of deep-fried balls of choux pastry served in syrup. *Glyká* (glee-KAH) is a kind of preserved candied fruit, made either with cherries, oranges, or figs, usually only made at village festivals. The Paphos district is famous for *loukoumia* (loo-koo-MYAH), or cubes of gelatin served in rosewater and covered with powdered sugar.

The Christmas season has its own array of special sweets and desserts. *Kourabiedes* (Koo-ra-beeds) are a type of shortbread made with almonds and sometimes flavored with rosewater. The dough is rolled into small balls, baked, and then rolled in powdered sugar. *Melomakarona* (mel-OH-ma-ka-ROH-na) are a type of Greek Christmas cookie made from honey and orange zest. They are stuffed with chopped dates and walnuts. On Christmas Eve, Cypriot women traditionally make loaves of *gennopitta,* sweet bread, which they decorate with a cross. The bread is then eaten on Christmas Day.

Baklavas is a dessert made of layers of filo pastry with nuts and honey.

FRESH PRODUCE

Guests at any dining table in Cyprus will be pleased by the amount of delicious, fresh, local produce. Cypriot fruit has a well-deserved reputation for tastiness. Fruit is sold in roadside stalls and in all the town bazaars. The warm climate and long growing season mean that Cypriot varieties tend to arrive at the market well before their counterparts in Europe, usually in April. In the south,

There are more than 2.5 million olive trees in Cyprus, and more than six hundred different varieties.

The Cypriot diet makes the most of the abundance of local produce.

strawberries are available all year round. Peaches, apricots, watermelon, and melons are also grown, as are plums and cherries. The many varieties of cherries grown on the foothills of the Troodos Mountains are delicious. Grapes appear in the early autumn, a by-product of the republic's successful wine industry. Apples, pears, figs, almonds, cherries, lemons, and oranges are also used in Cypriot cooking. Exotic fruit not native to Cyprus, such as avocados, bananas, and kiwis, have been introduced to the warmer corners of the Paphos district. Of course, olives from local groves and ripe juicy tomatoes are cultivated and take pride of place in many dishes.

BEVERAGES

A feature of island life since the Ottoman invasion is Turkish coffee—*kafés* (kah-FEHS) in Greek, *kahve* (kah-VEH) in Turkish. It is widely drunk on both sides of the partition, though in the south it is generally referred to as Greek or Cypriot coffee, despite its Turkish origins. The finely ground coffee is boiled, then poured straight into a small cup without filtering and drunk either with sugar or straight, leaving a muddy residue at the bottom of the cup. Ideally, it is said that coffee should be drunk dark. Since the arrival of settlers from Anatolia, the custom of brewing loose-leafed tea is becoming more popular in the villages of the north. Otherwise, tea is not a popular drink. Cyprus also produces its own mineral water—the Troodos and Kyrenia Mountains are both famous for their mountain springs, and some water is bottled and sold island-wide. Another popular drink sold by street vendors in Nicosia and Larnaca is *aïráni* (ah-ee-RAHN-ee), a refreshing concoction of diluted yogurt mixed with dried mint or oregano.

Traditionally, Cypriots only drink alcohol to accompany a meal. Wine is normally drunk with meals in the day, even for breakfast, while on special occasions beer and brandy will be drunk. The wine of the south is of a very high standard, owing to the island's near-perfect climate and the long tradition of winemaking. Most of the vineyards are on the slopes of the Troodos Mountains, around Paphos and Limassol. Today, Cyprus ranks fiftieth in the world in terms of total production of wine. This is a decline from a ranking of thirty-seventh a decade or so ago. Part of the reason for the lowered ranking is the increased production of some other nations, but repeated years of drought have also taken a toll on grape production. The wine industry continues to be an important part of Cyprus's economy and culture. Many Cypriot families are employed in the wine industry, and Cyprus's many varieties of wine are exported all over the world. The best varieties of wine include the dry white varieties Arsinoë, Palomino, and White Lady, and the Bellapais medium sparkling wine. Among red wines, Keo Othello and Rosella are common table wines. Commandaria is the most famous wine on the island and one of the oldest, having been made since the Middle Ages and possibly even earlier. It is produced using the age-old method of fermentation in open jars. The same jars are repeatedly used, so that each new batch contains a trace of traditional quality. Sherries are also produced. Local wine is also made in microwineries in the villages and monasteries of the Troodos, and drunk from the barrel.

Aïráni, made from yogurt, is a refreshing drink in the hot weather.

INTERNET LINKS

http://www.cyprus101.com/Cypriot_Food/page_1989934.html
Here you will find a list and descriptions of some of the most popular food and drink items in Cyprus.

https://www.cyprusisland.net/cyprus-cuisine
This is a comprehensive list of foods, drinks, and meals that are part of Cypriot cuisine.

PORK *SOUVLA* (GRILLED PORK SKEWERS)

2 pounds (1 kilogram) pork shoulder.
1 teaspoon ground oregano
½ teaspoon black pepper
1 tablespoon salt
2 tablespoons red wine vinegar
2 tablespoons olive oil

Before starting, make sure you ask an adult for help!

Cut the pork into 1-inch (2-centimeter) cubes. Place the cubes in a bowl. Pour the olive oil and red wine vinegar over the meat.

Sprinkle the salt, pepper, and oregano into the bowl and mix well. Cover the bowl and place in the refrigerator for 2 hours.

Thread the meat onto 12 skewers.

Ask your parents to help you grill for 15 minutes, turning the skewers frequently, until the meat is browned.

Serve with fresh lemon slices, a salad, tahini dip, and warm pita bread.

TAHINI DIP (SESAME DIP)

5 tablespoons tahini (sesame) paste
½ cup fresh lemon juice
2 cloves garlic
½ teaspoon salt
½ cup lukewarm water
3 tablespoons olive oil
1 tablespoon fresh chopped parsley

Place the tahini, lemon juice, garlic, and salt in a blender. Blend into a smooth cream. Add the water and olive oil and stir in.

Sprinkle the parsley on top and serve with warm pita bread.

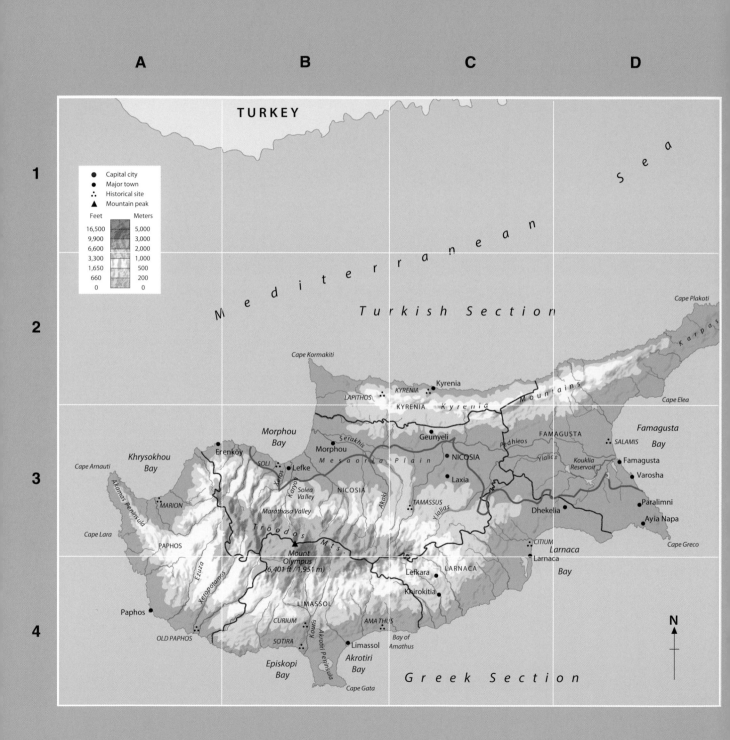

A **B** **C** **D**

TURKEY

1

Capital city
Major town
Historical site
Mountain peak

Feet | Meters
16,500 | 5,000
9,900 | 3,000
6,600 | 2,000
3,300 | 1,000
1,650 | 500
660 | 200
0 | 0

M e d i t e r r a n e a n   S e a

Cape Plakoti

T u r k i s h   S e c t i o n

2

Karpas

Cape Kormakiti

Kyrenia
KYRENIA
LAPITHOS
KYRENIA   *K y r e n i a   M o u n t a i n s*

Cape Elea

Morphou Bay

Khrysokhou Bay

Erenköy
SOLI
Morphou
Serakhis
Geunyeli
NICOSIA

FAMAGUSTA
SALAMIS
Famagusta Bay
Famagusta

3

Cape Arnauti
Atamas Peninsula
MARION
Lefke
Kenya
Solea Valley
NICOSIA
Mesaoria Plain
Laxia
Pedhieos
Yialias
Kouklia Reservoir
Varosha

Akaki
TAMASSUS
Yialias
Dhekelia
Paralimni

Cape Lara
PAPHOS
Marathasa Valley
Troodos *M t s.*
Mount Olympus
6,401 ft / 1,951 m)
CITIUM
Larnaca
Ayia Napa
Cape Greco

Ezuza
Xeropotamos
Lefkara
LARNACA
Larnaca
Larnaca Bay

Paphos
Khirokitia

LIMASSOL
N

4
OLD PAPHOS
CURIUM
Kouris
Garyllis
AMATHUS
SOTIRA
Limassol
Bay of Amathus
Akrotiri Peninsula
Episkopi Bay
Akrotiri Bay

G r e e k   S e c t i o n

Cape Gata

MAP OF CYPRUS

E

Cape Andreas

Peninsula

Akaki, B3
Akarnas Peninsula, A3
Akrotiri Bay, B4
Akrotiri Peninsula, B4
Amathus, B4
Ayia Napa, D3

Bay of Amathus, C4

Cape Andreas, E1
Cape Arnauti, A3
Cape Elea, D2
Cape Gata, B4
Cape Greco, D3
Cape Kormakiti, B2
Cape Lara, A3
Cape Plakoti, D2
Citium, C3
Curium, B4

Dhekelia, D3

Episkopi Bay, B4
Erenkoy, A3
Ezuza River, A3—A4

Famagusta (city), D3
Famagusta (region), C3, D3

Geunyeli, C3

Karpas Peninsula, D2, E2
Karyoti River, B3
Khirokitia, C4
Khrysokhou Bay, A3
Kouklia Reservior, D3

Kouris River, B4
Kyrenia (city), C2
Kyrenia (historical site), C2
Kyrenia (region), C2—C3
Kyrenia Mountains, B2, C2—C3, D2

Lapithos, B2
Larnaca Bay, C3—C4, D3
Larnaca (city), C3
Larnaca (region), C4
Laxia, C3
Lefkara, C4
Lefke, B3
Limassol (city), B4
Limassol (region), B4

Marathasa Valley, B3
Marion, A3
Mediterranean Sea, A1, B1—B2, C1—C2, D1—D2
Mesaoria Plain, B3
Morphou Bay, B3
Morphou, B3
Mount Olympus, B3

Nicosia (city), C3
Nicosia (region), B3

Old Paphos, A4

Paphos (city), A4
Paphos (region), A3
Paralimni, D3
Pedhieos River, C3, C3

Salamis, D3
Serakhis River, B3
Solea Valley, B3
Soli, B3
Sotira, B4

Tamassus, C3
Troodos Mountains, A3—A4, B3—B4, C3
Turkey, A1, B1, C1

Varosha, D3

Xeropotamos River, A4, B3
Xeros River, B3

Yialias River, C3, D3

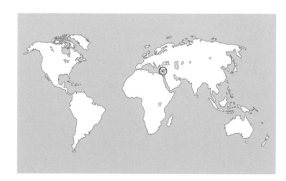

ECONOMIC CYPRUS

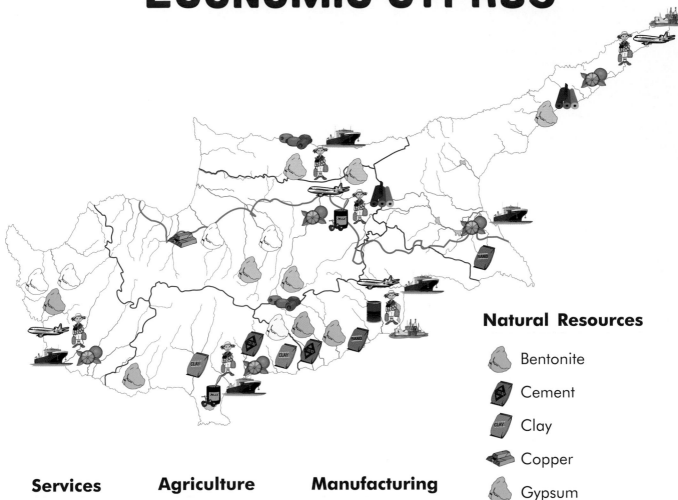

Natural Resources

- Bentonite
- Cement
- Clay
- Copper
- Gypsum
- Limestone
- Marble & Alasbaster
- Petroleum
- Pyrite
- Sand
- Stone

Services

-  Airport
- Port
- Tourism

Agriculture

- Citrus
- Olive

Manufacturing

- Food processing
- Ship repair
- Textiles

ABOUT THE ECONOMY

OVERVIEW

Area under government control:
Cyprus adopted the Euro as its national currency on January 1, 2008. The service sector accounts for 86.8 percent of GDP. Cyprus today has a strong economy, although growth rate can fluctuate due to its overreliance on tourism. As a result of the global economic crisis in 2009, Cyprus's prosperity suffered, as construction and tourism slowed in the face of reduced foreign demand. However, the economy has bounced back at an impressive rate, and the nation has almost fully recovered to its pre-crisis state.

Turkish Cyprus:
The Turkish Cypriot economy has approximately 40 percent of the per-capita GDP of the south. The economy and labor force are more reliant on agriculture and industry than the south. The Turkish Cypriots are still dependent on investment from the Turkish government.

CURRENCY

Area under government control, 1 US dollar = 0.86 euros (2018 estimate); Turkish Cyprus, 1 US dollar = 6.43 Turkish new lira (2018)

GROSS DOMESTIC PRODUCT (GDP)

$31.59 billion (2017 estimate)

GDP PER CAPITA

Area under government control, $37,000 (2017 estimate); Turkish Cyprus, $15,109 (2014 estimate)

GDP BY SECTOR

Area under government control: agriculture, 2.3 percent; industry, 11 percent; services, 86.8 percent (2017); Turkish Cyprus: agriculture, 6.2 percent; industry, 35.1 percent; services, 58.7 percent (2012)

UNEMPLOYMENT RATE

Area under government control, 11.8 percent (2017 estimate); Turkish Cyprus, 8.3 percent (2015 estimate)

MAIN TRADE PARTNERS

Area under government control: Greece, Italy, China, Libya, Greece, Norway, UK; Turkish Cyprus: Turkey, European Union; direct trade between Turkish Cyprus and the area under government control remains limited.

MAIN EXPORTS

Area under government control: Citrus, potatoes, pharmaceuticals, cement, and clothing; Turkish Cyprus: Citrus, dairy, potatoes, textiles

CULTURAL CYPRUS

The Tombs of the Kings
A UNESCO World Heritage site, the "Tombs of the Kings" are situated close to the sea in the northwestern necropolis of Paphos. They owe their name to their size and splendor and not because royalty was buried there. They are rock cut and date to the Hellenistic and early Roman periods. Some of them imitate the houses of the living, with the rooms (here the burial chambers) opening onto a peristyle atrium.

Khirokitia
Inscribed as a UNESCO World Heritage site in 1998, the Neolithic settlement of Khirokitia (or Choirokoitia) in the district of Larnaca, occupied from the seventh to the fourth millennium BCE, is one of the most important prehistoric sites in the eastern Mediterranean. Only part of the site has been excavated, but it serves as an exceptional archaeological site for study, both now and in the future.

Kyrenia and Kyrenia Castle
Kyrenia was founded in the tenth century BCE by Achaean settlers and was for many centuries one of the ten kingdoms of Cyprus. The town remained a minor port under Ottoman rule. Under British rule, the harbor and quay were built. The impressive Kyrenia Castle, at the eastern end of the harbor, was built in the seventh century CE by the Byzantines in order to protect the city against Arab raids. Just behind the harbor is the Agha Cafer Pasha mosque, constructed in 1580 during the Ottoman period. Beside the mosque lies the Hasan Kavizade Huseyin Efendi fountain, built in 1841.

Nicosia
Nicosia lies roughly at the center of the island and is the only capital city in the world to remain divided by force. It has a rich history that can be traced back to the Bronze Age. It is a magnificent city with a royal palace and many churches. Today, it blends its historic past brilliantly with the bustle of a modern city. The old walled city, enclosed by sixteenth-century Venetian walls, is dotted with museums, ancient churches, and medieval buildings.

Painted Churches in the Troodos Region
Inscribed as a UNESCO World Heritage site in 1985, the Troodos region in the districts of Nicosia and Limassol is characterized by one of the largest groups of churches and monasteries of the former Byzantine Empire. The complex of monuments, all richly decorated with murals, provides an overview of Byzantine and post-Byzantine painting.

Famagusta, Salamis, and Enkomi
Famagusta possesses the deepest harbor and is one of the most fortified ports in the Mediterranean. Nearby are two ancient towns, Enkomi and Salamis. Enkomi was one of the first settlements in eastern Cyprus. The spectacular ruins at Salamis include a magnificent amphitheater, Roman baths, a gymnasium, and royal tombs.

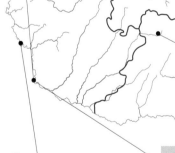

Maa-Palaeokastro Settlement
Maa-Palaeokastro is a settlement on the western coast of the island close to Coral Bay. Its imposing defensive walls were always exposed and gave the site its name of "Palaeokastro" ("the old castle"). This area was settled by the first Mycenaean Greeks who arrived on the island around 1200 BCE, after the fall of the Mycenaean kingdoms in mainland Greece. The site is well known for its fortification walls.

Paphos
Paphos is situated along the southwestern coast. It is the mythical birthplace of Aphrodite, the Greek goddess of love and beauty. In Greco-Roman times, Paphos was the island's capital, and it is famous for the remains of the Roman governor's palace, where extensive, beautiful mosaics can be found. The town is included in the official UNESCO World Heritage list.

Limassol
Limassol is situated in the south of the island. It is Cyprus's main industrial and maritime area and also the second-largest town of the country. Places of interest include the old city; Berengaria Castle, the place where Richard the Lionheart married Berengaria; Kolossi Castle; the ancient city of Curium and its still functioning theater; the ruins of Amathunta (also called Amathus); and many other archeological spots scattered around the city.

OFFICIAL NAME
Republic of Cyprus
The Turkish Cypriot community refers to itself as the Turkish Republic of Northern Cyprus (TRNC).

NATIONAL FLAG
White with a copper-colored silhouette of the island above two green crossed olive branches that symbolize the hope for peace and reconciliation between the Greek and Turkish communities.
The Turkish Republic of Northern Cyprus flag has a white field with narrow horizontal red stripes a small distance from the top and bottom edges, with a red crescent and a red five-pointed star in the middle.

NATIONALITY
Cypriot, Turkish Cypriot

CAPITAL
Nicosia (Lefkosia)

LAND AREA
3,568 square miles (9,241 sq km)

POPULATION
1,221,549 (July 2017 estimate)

ADMINISTRATIVE DISTRICTS
6 districts: Famagusta, Kyrenia, Larnaca, Limassol, Nicosia, Paphos; Turkish Cypriot area's administrative divisions include Kyrenia, all but a small part of Famagusta, and small parts of Nicosia (Lefkosia)

LANGUAGES (OFFICIAL)
Greek, Turkish

ETHNIC GROUPS
Greek 98.8 percent, other 1 percent (2011 census). Note that these statistics only represent the Republic of Cyprus and therefore omit many Turkish Cypriots.

MAJOR RELIGIONS
Greek Orthodox 89.1 percent, Roman Catholic 2.9 percent, Protestant 2 percent, Muslim 1.8 percent, other (includes Maronite and Armenian Apostolic) 4.2 percent (2011 census, based on Republic of Cyprus only).

BIRTH RATE
11.3 births/1,000 population
(2017 estimate)

INFANT MORTALITY RATE
7.9 deaths/1,000 live births
(2017 estimate)

LIFE EXPECTANCY
78.8 years; male: 76 years; female: 81.8 years (2017 estimate)

TIMELINE

IN CYPRUS	IN THE WORLD

8th century BCE
Cyprus conquered and unified by the Assyrian Empire under Sargon II.

294 BCE
Ptolemy I of Macedonia, the ruler of Egypt, takes over Cyprus.

45 CE
Saint Paul preaches in Cyprus, accompanied by Saint Barnabas.

116–117 CE
The Roman Empire reaches its greatest extent, under Emperor Trajan (98–117).

1191
King Richard I takes over Cyprus. He soon gives control to the Lusignans.

1206–1368
Genghis Khan unifies the Mongols and starts conquest of the world. At its height, the Mongol Empire under Kublai Khan stretches from China to Persia and parts of Europe and Russia.

1530
Beginning of transatlantic slave trade organized by the Portuguese in Africa.

1570
The Ottomans invade Cyprus.

1789–1799
The French Revolution.

1878
The British military occupy and administer Cyprus by mutual agreement with the Ottoman government.

1914–1918
World War I.

1925
Cyprus becomes a British Crown colony.

1931
Violent protests by Greek Cypriots demanding union with mainland Greece.

1939–1945
World War II.

1955
National Organization of Cypriot Fighters (EOKA), Greek Cypriot activists and guerrilla fighters, begin a bombing campaign to support their push for union with Greece.

1958
Turkish Cypriots, alarmed by British conciliation, begin demands for partition.

1960
Cyprus becomes independent.

IN CYPRUS	IN THE WORLD
1963 • Interethnic fighting erupts after political disagreements.	• **1966** The Chinese Cultural Revolution.
1974 • President Makarios is overthrown in a military-backed coup. The coup is put down and Makarios returns to power. After talks break down, Turkey lands forty thousand troops in the north.	
1983 • The north declares itself an independent state, the Turkish Republic of Northern Cyprus (TRNC).	• **1986** Nuclear power disaster at Chernobyl in Ukraine. • **1991** Breakup of the Soviet Union. • **1997** Hong Kong is returned to China. • **2001** Terrorists crash planes in New York, Washington, DC, and Pennsylvania.
2004 • Cyprus is admitted to the European Union.	
2008 • Dimitris Christofias becomes Cyprus's first communist president.	• **2008** Earthquake in Sichuan province, China, kills thousands.
2009 • National Unity Party wins parliamentary elections in northern Cyprus.	• **2009** Financial crisis in much of Europe worsens.
2010 • Pro-independence candidate Derviş Eroğlu wins northern leadership race.	• **2010** Earthquake in Haiti kills many. • **2011** Japanese tsunami causes accidents at Fukushima Daiichi Nuclear Power Plant. Thousands are killed.
2012 • A planned reunification conference is canceled. The financial crisis in Greece extends to Cyprus.	
2013 • Nicos Anastasiades is elected president.	• **2014** An Ebola outbreak in West Africa kills thousands.
2016 • Leaders of the republic and the north deliver a joint New Year's television address.	• **2016** First Olympic Games to be held in South America take place in Rio de Janeiro, Brazil.
2018 • Nicos Anastasiades is elected to a second term as president.	

GLOSSARY

affedersiniz (ahf-ehd-ehr-sih-NIH Z)
Means "sorry" or "I beg your pardon" in Turkish.

aïráni (ah-ee-RAHN -ee)
A refreshing concoction of diluted yogurt mixed with dried mint or oregano.

bilgi (bihl-GEE)
Means "knowledge" in Turkish.

bir dakika (bih dah-kih-KAH)
Means "wait a minute" in Turkish.

cepken (chep-KEHN)
Short, embroidered vests worn by Turkish Cypriot men.

dhrepanin (threh-PAH -neen)
A traditional Cypriot "sickle dance."

enosis
Greek for "union," refers to the movement to unite Greece and Cyprus as a single country.

karpasitiko (karp-ahs-IHT -ih-koh)
Popular traditional dress worn by Greek Cypriot women.

kartchilamas (gar-chee-LAH -mahs)
A popular Cypriot dance performed by facing pairs of male and female dancers.

laoudo (LAH -oo-doh)
A long-necked flute.

misafir (mihs-ah-FEER)
Turkish word for "guest."

ne haber (neh hah-BER)
Means "how are you?" in Turkish.

pitharia (PIH -thah-ree-ah)
Large, traditional Cypriot earthenware containers used for storing olives, wine, and olive oil.

pó-pó-pó (POH -poh-poh)
A Greek expression of dismay.

shalvar (shahl-VAH R)
Baggy trousers worn by Turkish Cypriot men and women.

sigá sigá (see-GAH see-GAH)
Means "slow down and relax" in Greek.

syrtos (SEE -tohs) and mandra (MAHN -drah)
Traditional Cypriot dances.

taksim (tahk-SIH M)
A Turkish word meaning "partition."

ti néa (tee NEH -ah)
Means "what's new" in Greek.

tzouras (TZOW-ras)
A stringed musical instrument resembling a lute.

yá sou (YA soo)
Means "health to you" in Greek.

FOR FURTHER INFORMATION

BOOKS

Cyprus. DK Eyewitness Travel Guide. London, UK: Dorling Kindersley, 2016.

Gürsoy, Kristina, and Lavinia Neville Smith. *Northern Cyprus*. Landmark Visitors Guide. London, UK: Landmark Publishing Ltd., 2009.

Koumi, Andreas. *The Cypriot*. London, UK: Dexter Haven, 2009.

Lee, Jessica. *Cyprus*. Lonely Planet Country Guide. Oakland, CA: Lonely Planet Publications, 2018.

Mallinson, William. *Cyprus: A Modern History*. London, UK: I. B. Tauris & Co. Ltd., 2008.

The Rough Guide to Cyprus. London, UK: Rough Guides Publishing, 2016.

WEBSITES

http://www.birdlifecyprus.org

https://www.chooseyourcyprus.com

https://www.cia.gov/library/publications/the-world-factbook/geos/print_cy.html

http://www.cyprus.gov.cy

https://cypruswildlife.com

http://www.kypros.org/Cyprus/environment.html

https://www.paphoslife.com

http://www.unicef.org/infobycountry/cyprus.html

FILMS

Akamas. Artimages and Hellenic Radio & Television, 2006.

Cities of the World: Cyprus. Shepherd Entertainment, 2009.

Ian Cross, Globe Trekker: Cyprus and Crete. Pilot Productions, 2008.

Shadows and Faces. Maraton Filmcilik, 2010.

The Last Homecoming. Avra Productions and Cyprus Broadcasting Corporation, 2008.

World Destinations: Cyprus. Video House International, 2010.

BIBLIOGRAPHY

Ciesla, William M. "Forests and Forest Protection in Cyprus." *Forestry Chronicle* 80, no. 1 (2004).

Drake, Catherine. "Why Cyprus Is Europe's Most Exciting Art Hub Right Now." Artnet, March 14, 2017. https://news.artnet.com/art-world/cyprus-art-scene-887609.

Durrell, Lawrence. *Bitter Lemons.* London, UK: Axios Press, 2009.

Edbury, Peter W. *The Kingdom of Cyprus and the Crusades, 1191—1374.* Cambridge, UK: Cambridge University Press, 1993.

Gani, Martin. *Cyprus Revisited.* Independently published, 2018.

Hatzopoulos, Militiades B. *Betwixt and Between.* Nicosia, Cyprus: Armida Publications, 2014.

Ker-Lindsay, James. *The Cyprus Problem: What Everyone Needs to Know.* Oxford, UK: Oxford University Press, 2011.

Kermeliotis, Teo. "All You Need to Know About Cyprus Presidential Election." Al Jazeera, January 28, 2018. https://www.aljazeera.com/news/2018/01/cyprus-presidential-election-180126223607469.html.

Langdale, Allan. *In a Contested Realm: An Illustrated Guide to the Archaeology and Historical Architecture of Northern Cyprus.* London, UK: Grimsay Press, 2012.

Polo, Marco. *Cyprus Marco Polo Pocket Guide.* London, UK: Marco Polo Travel Publishing, 2018.

Steele, Philippa M. *Writing and Society in Ancient Cyprus.* Cambridge, UK: Cambridge University Press, 2018.

Varnava, Andrekos, and Hubert Faustmann, ed. *Reunifying Cyprus: The Annan Plan and Beyond.* New York: I. B. Tauris, 2011.

INDEX

INDEX